Francis Dwyer

**On Seats and Saddles**

Bits and Bitting and the Prevention and Cure of Restiveness in Horses

Francis Dwyer

**On Seats and Saddles**
*Bits and Bitting and the Prevention and Cure of Restiveness in Horses*

ISBN/EAN: 9783744648332

Printed in Europe, USA, Canada, Australia, Japan

Cover: Foto ©Andreas Hilbeck / pixelio.de

More available books at **www.hansebooks.com**

'ON

# SEATS AND SADDLES

# BITS AND BITTING

ETC.

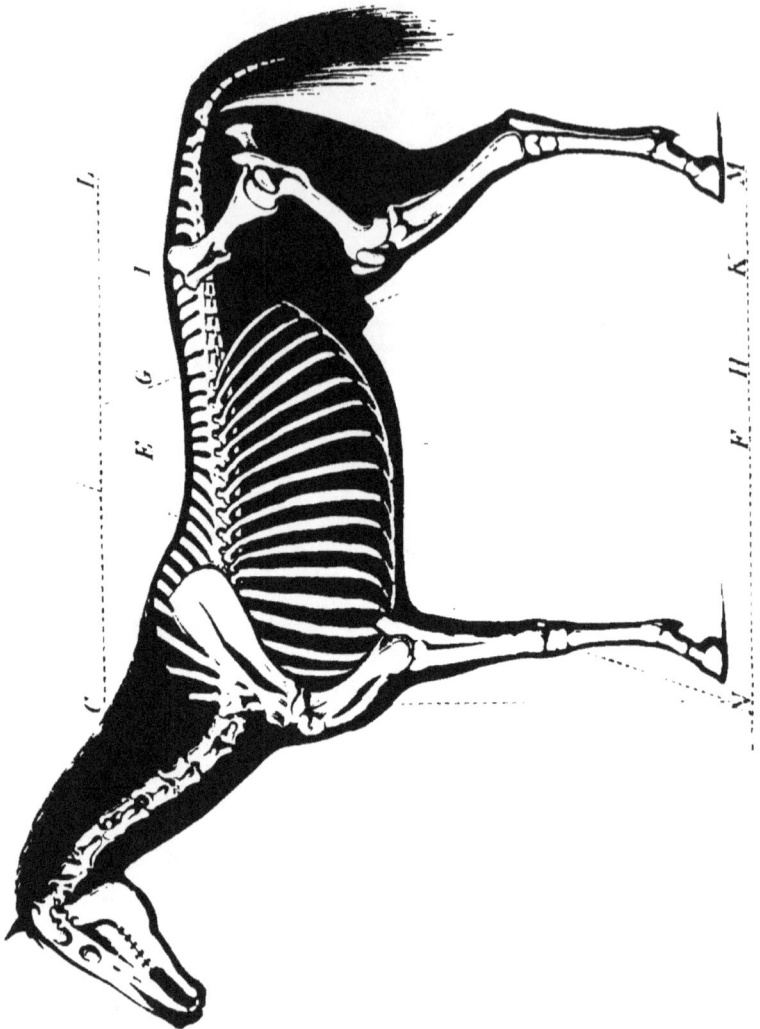

ON

# SEATS AND SADDLES

# BITS AND BITTING

AND

## THE PREVENTION AND CURE OF

## RESTIVENESS IN HORSES

BY

## FRANCIS DWYER

MAJOR OF HUSSARS IN THE IMPERIAL AUSTRIAN SERVICE

"Vis consili expers mole ruit suâ."
—HORACE, *Carmin.*, Lib. III. Ode iv.

## WILLIAM BLACKWOOD AND SONS

### EDINBURGH AND LONDON

### MDCCCLXVIII

# TABLE OF CONTENTS.

# PART I.

### SEATS AND SADDLES.

## CHAPTER I.

#### THE FRAMEWORK OF THE HORSE CONSIDERED FROM A MECHANICAL POINT OF VIEW.

## CHAPTER II.

#### THE SADDLE, AND ITS INFLUENCE ON THE SEAT.

## CHAPTER III.

### SEATS.

## CHAPTER IV.

### THE MILITARY SEAT.

---

# PART II.

## BITS AND BITTING.

### CHAPTER I.

#### GENERAL PRINCIPLES.

### CHAPTER II.

#### THE NECK—THE HEAD—THE MOUTH—THE TONGUE— CARRIAGE—FEELING.

/

# PART III.

## CHAPTER III.

### SPECIAL FORMS OF RESTIVENESS.

# LIST OF PLATES.

# INTRODUCTORY CHAPTER.

It may be well, at starting, to state the objects with which this little book has been brought before the public interested in horses, and at the same time, in order to prevent misapprehension, to say, that the author has not the slightest intention of setting up any one kind of seat or style of riding as a model for all riders. On the contrary, he is fully persuaded that each of these has its own merits, and, as our French neighbours would say, its own *raison d'être*—that is to say, has been adopted for good and sufficient reasons, so far as each individual rider possessed an insight into the true essentials of the case, and has been able to distinguish these from what is merely matter of fashion or supposed convenience.

Some men, and these are the naturally good or born riders, possess the sort of knowledge in question instinctively, and frequently without being able to account either to themselves or others for the way in which they have acquired it, or give satisfactory reasons for the adoption of their methods. Such men are most usually, although not invariably, of the peculiar build,

A

unnecessary to describe, which combines strength and vigour with lightness and dexterity; and must possess in all cases that happy admixture of courage, prompt decision, patience, and perseverance, that constitute the rider's temperament, and which arrive at their greatest perfection when coupled with an unselfish love of that noblest and most beautiful animal the horse. It is only necessary to put a man of this sort into the saddle and he becomes at once a rider; just as another becomes a good shot, and a third an expert angler, almost from the moment a gun or a rod is placed in their hands.

But all men are not so gifted; whole nations, indeed, have been at various periods of the world's history characterised as born riders; but it will be found, on examination, that in these instances unmixed race, resulting in great uniformity of stature, build, and temperament, combined with what we are pleased to term a low degree of civilisation, prevailed to a much greater extent than amongst ourselves. It would be invidious, and moreover unnecessary, for the object we have in view, to enter into a minute comparison in this respect of our own population with others of ancient or modern times. As regards most if not all of those moral qualities that we have stated to be typical of the rider temperament, we stand confessedly very high in the scale, leaving altogether aside all that England has done for the breeding of horses: moreover, we have amongst us a much greater proportion of men who can ride *tant bien que mal* than any other civilised nation; in fact, the class of men that ride for pleasure or convenience is with us very large, whereas everywhere else it is very small, almost minute; for the equestrian nations that still exist in different parts of the world mount their horses as a means of gaining and maintaining their existence much more frequently than for mere pleasure.

This is, however, precisely what brings into the saddle a great number of people who do not belong to the class of born riders, or have perhaps neither the time, opportunity, nor desire to do more than enjoy a pleasant ride when they can, and who are therefore content to depend on others, who are paid for doing it, to put this within their reach. That this luxury is, however, not always attainable even to a long purse, many a man can testify; and the causes of failure are frequently sufficiently obvious to professional riders, although seldom pointed out by them, for very cogent reasons. It must be confessed, indeed, that it is most usually a very thankless office to offer any man that rides anything like advice, however well meant and sound, on anything concerning his horse, bridle, saddle, or seat. The great majority would much more patiently tolerate very decided expressions of doubt as to their mental or moral qualifications, if only conveyed with a certain amount of tact, than the slightest imputation of want of knowledge or skill in things pertaining to horsemanship.

And yet there exist very incontestable evidences that a great amount of unskilfulness, to use a mild term, in the matter of riding does really exist amongst us. We have the best horses in the world, and those whose build and temper are most peculiarly adapted for riding purposes; notwithstanding which, the proportion of animals with broken knees and other injuries to their limbs is infinitely greater than anywhere else that we know of. No doubt we demand a greater amount of hard work from our horses than other people ; still broken knees are the opprobrium of the rider, and point very evidently to great ignorance or total disregard of the very simple mechanical principles that govern the motion of a quadruped with or without a burden on its back. Every one knows that the best-constructed form or chair may be upset by sitting awkwardly on it and setting the laws of gravitation at defiance ; whilst few people who have knocked down their valuable horses by precisely the same process seem to be in the least aware of what they have really done : " the brute stumbled and broke both his knees," is the only explanation they are capable of affording ; of course it is never their own fault.

Again, how many horses, especially young ones, are made restive, and become plungers, bolters, or rearers, through the intolerable pain occasioned by bits that are wholly unsuited to their mouths, and sometimes fitter for a rhinoceros than so sensitive and delicate an animal as the horse. Many a curb, stringhalt, and spavin, are originated by the use, or rather abuse, of bits whose lever power is so excessive that it is impossible to regulate their action, not to mention the very numerous instances in which bits are placed in such a position in the horse's mouth as to act on the animal's head in exactly the opposite direction to that intended by the rider, as shall be hereafter explained, and thus, in conjunction with the misplaced burden of the rider, assist in throwing down the bearer.

It is well known that a very great and constantly-increasing number of English saddle-horses are annually exported to Berlin, Vienna, Paris, and other great Continental cities, and many of these are there sold at prices perfectly remunerative to the dealers, but which are much lower than animals of equally good figure and proportions command with ease in the English market. This was for a time a puzzle to the Continentals, and even to some amateur dealers, who made bad speculations in consequence. By-and-by it was discovered that a great majority of these splendid animals were either more or less restive, or at least " difficult," as the phrase goes. Being frequently purchased by military officers of superior rank, they were naturally put into the riding-schools, where they gave so much trouble that many professionals were led to believe that English horses were incapable of any high degree of school-training. Others who were more judicious found it impossible to reconcile the well-known docility of the English breed with the fractiousness and intractability of these exported specimens, and came to the very sound conclusion that the fault lay, not in the breed, but in the previous injudicious handling of these individuals. Baucher, the French riding-master, founded his great reputation,—which, by the way, has been much exaggerated,—on his successful conversion of the celebrated Partisan—an English horse that was sold for a song, because nobody could manage him—into a first-rate and most docile school-horse. Some of the Germans, however, decided the question in a still more positive manner, by buying young high-bred horses in England that had never been backed ; and Seeger, Von Oeynhausen, and other first-rate authorities, now all state that English horses are just as capable of high training as all others, and more so than the Arabians, who have a very peculiar trot.

It is incontestable that the English, as a nation, possess in a high degree the physical and moral qualifications that go to make good riders. Where, then, can the fault lie? Evidently in something connected with the mechanism employed in enabling the horse to carry its rider, and the rider to maintain his seat and preserve the mastery over his bearer; in other words, something *peculiar in saddles and seats, bits and bitting.*

It will perhaps seem to many persons impossible, or at least improbable, that mere saddles and bridles, or the manner in which they are adjusted to the horse's body, can produce such very material results as those suggested here. Well, it does seem strange; but let us listen, before passing judgment on the case, to some documentary evidence bearing upon it. On the 20th May 1859, the French cavalry had in Piedmont 9008 effective horses, increased subsequently by the arrival of a whole brigade (Perouse), so that on the 24th June (Solferino), the total number borne on the lists was 10,206.* But it subsequently transpired, from the report of the Cavalry Commission ordered by Marshal Randon to inquire into the causes of the tear and wear of horses during the campaign, that, on the day of that decisive battle, not more than about 3500 horses were really fit for service, the remainder having been disabled by less than one month's marching; for, with the exception of one or two squadrons that fought at Magenta, the French cavalry was never under fire up to the 24th June, and an immense proportion of these had been rendered unserviceable by the *saddle* and other portions of the equipment.

* 'Campagne de l'Empereur Napoleon III. en Italie en 1859' (official).

Most of us, too, have heard of what happened to that portion of our own cavalry that was employed in the reconnoitring expedition into the Dobrudscha. A proverb current amongst the Continental military men says, that more men are put *hors de combat* by the calfskin (the knapsack) than by either bullet or bayonet; and there seems good reason to believe that the pigskin stands in the same fatal relation to horses.

There is no lack of books in which very full and particular descriptions of model seats on horseback may be found, nor of riding-masters who both know how to sit a horse themselves, and impart to their pupils their own particular method. But this will not answer the purpose; for there exist not only a certain number of typical seats, more or less suited to various ends—as racing, hunting, the cavalry service, &c., all of which, as has been said, have their peculiar justification—but there is also a great variety in the build of horses, and especially in the relative power of their fore and hind quarters, which demands consideration, if we would avoid the serious and but too common error of using up one set of members prematurely whilst leaving the others intact. For instance, nothing is more frequent amongst ourselves than to see horses otherwise perfectly sound, irreparably ruined in the fore legs.

Moreover, there exists an equal variety in the build of the riders, which also requires consideration. Dr Heavysterne cannot be expected to sit his horse as Mr Threadpaper can do, nor a well " split up " man like one that is built on the lines of an otter; nevertheless there is no reason why each and all of them should not sit *well* and judiciously, though their seats must be necessarily different. There is only one class of riders from which one must and can demand a great degree of uniformity, namely, cavalry. The necessity arises from the existence of a special and narrowly-defined object being to be attained—the possibility, from the fact of both men and horses being selected with reference to this very object. But even here a certain margin is inevitable. It is not possible to make the Indo-Germanic Prussians, Bavarians, French, English, or Irish, sit on horseback exactly like the Mongolian Magyars and Turks, or the Semitic Arabs. Professor Max Müller and the author of the Adamites seem to have overlooked this interesting fact. Still, the mutual relations of the frameworks of the man and of the horse are such as to admit of one general principle being set up, and this *must* be adhered to as closely as possible if the real end and object are not to be sacrificed to fashion or prejudice.

It is more difficult to lay down anything like a principle for the guidance of that large class of men who ride simply for pleasure, convenience, or health. To one considerable section of them the notion of sitting their horses as a riding-master is supposed to do would be simply disgusting; it would look like an affectation, a sort of thing to which well-bred gentlemen have a great objection. They can afford to ride tolerably safe horses, and depend on their saddles and groom to a great extent for the convenience and comfort of their seat. These important functionaries must be often sadly puzzled how to insure this, and would be probably often delighted to find their employer capable of giving them some intelligible hint on which they might exercise their ingenuity and *savoir faire* with a decent chance of success.

The next section comprises those who are indifferent to appearances, and merely desire to ride safely and comfortably. As regards the latter point, we may refer them to what has been just said; and as to the matter of safety, this will be perhaps better attained by some knowledge of where the danger lies, and how it may be avoided, than by a practical experience of it in the shape of a fall.

Others again, although they never followed a hound, nor are likely to do so, adopt what they believe to be "a hunting seat" merely because it is a prominent type, and therefore caught their eye more readily than the chaos that presented itself in all other directions. Many of them would doubtless adopt with equal readiness some other form that promised equal or greater security and convenience, especially if they should happen to discover, by the aid of a looking-glass, that their copy is somewhat too much of a caricature.

The aim of this little treatise is therefore, by appealing to the intelligence, common sense, and good feeling of all riding men, to enable each to discover for himself what best suits his own peculiar case, and will put him in a position to make the best and the most of every horse he may have to ride, in the safest manner, so far at least as the matters herein treated are concerned. The intention is to refrain from all dogmatism and authoritative assertions, and merely present general principles, derived from mechanical laws that admit of no controversy, showing their inevitable bearing on the most important points, and leaving the reader as much as possible to form his own judgment independently, and arrive at a practical application for himself. The work is therefore not intended to represent a

treatise on equitation or the art of riding, but merely
to be a plain and easily intelligible exposition of the
mechanical problems connected with the case of a
quadruped serving as a bearer to a biped—in other
words, of a horse under its rider.

The plan to be adopted will be, first, as regards
" Seats and Saddles," as follows : The horse's skeleton
is a framework forming the basis of the living machine
we employ as a bearer ; it is therefore necessary to
know something of its construction, less from an ana-
tomical than a mechanical point of view.   The principles involved are very simple, and familiar to most
people in one way or the other, regarding chiefly equilibrium—that is to say, such a distribution of a weight
with reference to its supports as insures stability, or,
in other words, prevents its upsetting or falling ; also
something about levers.

The chief weight to be carried by the machine is, of
course, the rider, whose seat should therefore be so adjusted as not to interfere with the free action of the
bearer and the preservation of its stability and equilibrium.   But as the seat depends to a great extent on
the saddle, it becomes necessary to examine, in the
first place, the general principles of construction of
this mechanical contrivance, by means of which the
twofold object of securing the free action of the horse
and the safety of the rider may be best attained.   This
will be found to depend partly on the absolute amount
of surface coming in contact on the one hand with the
horse's back, on the other with the rider's seat ; partly
on the way in which the weight of the latter is adjusted on the saddle—that is to say, whether it presses
more on one part than another, and consequently,

chiefly on one or two points of the horse's back, or whether it be distributed equably over the whole surface in contact with the latter,—in other words, what part of the saddle the rider should occupy in order to secure the objects he has in view, as stated above. It will further depend on the general shape of those parts of its under and upper surfaces that come in contact with the horse's back and rider's seat respectively, which, of course, includes the question of its proper place, its mode of attachment—that is to say, where and how the girths should be fixed—and the causes of its displacement, which depend partly on its own shape favouring, partly on the rider's seat producing, lever action, which again depends to a great extent on the exact point from which the stirrups are suspended.

This will furnish data for an estimate, not so much of the relative value of different kinds of seats —which would only divert attention from the real object, and provoke controversy—as of their absolute fitness for the particular purpose they are intended to fulfil; and will also afford an opportunity of pointing out the danger of exaggerations, and the gross absurdity of applying a style of riding more or less specially adapted to one purpose, to others that have no analogy with it ; in fact, it will be shown that different styles of riding are not only inevitable but legitimate, because the ends to be attained vary considerably. But at the same time, although the general principles may be adapted to circumstances, they can never be absolutely violated with impunity. Let each particular style of riding be as perfect in itself as possible without being made antagonistic to others, or losing sight of the general conditions that apply to all

without exception.   There is a great value in schools ;
for, making due allowance for individuality, they enable
us to form a correct estimate of what the scholars can
do.   For instance, in "welters" we impose penalties on
professional jocks, because we know that they have
been trained in a certain school ; whereas we have no
standard of comparison for gentlemen-riders.

It is proposed to illustrate this portion of the book
with drawings of horsemen, representing various styles
of European and Asiatic riding, taken from portraits,
photographs, and pictures executed by artists who had
no preconceived theories to bolster up, and picked
nearly at random from such materials as were available.
They will be found to confirm, in a remarkable manner,
the truth of the general principles laid down, as well
by their discrepancies as their points of resemblance,
and will no doubt prove interesting to many readers in
other respects.

The European cavalry soldier is compelled to put on
his horse's back, in addition to his own weight and
that of the saddle, the extra burden of a huge pack of
things forming his kit.   It is obvious that the most
careful adjustment of the rider and saddle to the general equilibrium of himself and horse will avail little if
the balance be destroyed from the moment the pack is
put on ; nor will it do to make this merely a counterpoise to the rider, because he is frequently required to
ride either in an empty saddle or with various amounts
of pack, therefore the equilibrium must be at all times
maintainable, whatever the absolute weight may be.
The neglect of this is one of the main causes of the
sore-back disasters that usually occur at the commencement of a campaign, and, to the great astonishment

of the uninitiated, frequently nearly disappear in the further course of it.

There is another great difference between the conditions under which the soldier and the civilian mount their horses, the former being compelled to ride with one hand, and have the other free to use his weapons ; besides, his life frequently depends on a rapid change of direction at various degrees of speed, and which he must be able to effect without great effort.  The way in which the pack is placed on the saddle has much to do with this, as will appear when we come to the subject of " Bits and Bitting."   All these matters shall be treated in a separate chapter, and illustrated by figures.

The second part of the work is devoted to " Bits and Bitting."   There is much more in this than most people may be willing to believe.   A ship with a damaged or badly-constructed and ill-fitting rudder is not more awkward and difficult to manage than a horse with a bit that is not perfectly adapted to his mouth and his whole frame, or which has been ill placed.   It will be necessary here to refer again to the horse's skeleton, and point out the beautiful series of levers, and the wonderful lever action, by means of which, in conjunction with the seat and legs of the rider, his will may be conveyed from his little finger through the reins, bit, head, and neck of the horse, down to the very last joint of its hind legs, in the, to the animal, most unmistakable and peremptory manner.

Although bitting finds its place here after saddling, this is not because of its being a secondary consideration, but rather because no man can have a light hand, or, in fact, use any bit properly, unless he have so steady and close a seat as to put all suspicion of what is technically termed "rein-riding" out of the question. This self-same rein-riding—that is, the depending to any extent on the reins for maintaining the seat—is but too common, and a frequent cause of restiveness in horses, and no end of disasters to riders. It must be admitted that a certain exaggerated method of rising in the stirrups and totally abandoning all contact with the saddle, in which Sunday and holiday riders so much delight, conduces very directly to this. Of course no good rider cares to perform this description of equestrian antic; still it is sufficiently common, even amongst men who should know better, to demand attention, and is noticed here for the sake of illustrating the close connection that exists between bitting and saddling.

The mechanical principles on which the action of the bit depends form the first subject of inquiry. Then we shall have to examine into the internal and external conformation of the horse's mouth to which this instrument is applied; we shall thence be enabled to deduce the dimensions of the several parts of the bit, and also ascertain its proper place. Some few of these dimensions are nearly constant—others, again, are variable, and the proper means for ascertaining them shall be pointed out. The use of the snaffle, the running-reins, the nose-band, and other contrivances, demands some attention, as also the real and supposed advantages of various kinds of bits.

The third and last part of the book is devoted to the "Prevention and Cure of Restiveness." Violent measures are seldom successful for the latter purpose, and more likely to produce than to prevent insubordination. In fact, what is generally required is a com-

plete course of re-training, under circumstances different from those under which the restiveness is usually
exhibited.   The question then arises, On what system
this re-training should be undertaken—the usual English one, or some modification of the school method?
The first named, taken alone, is inadequate to the
purpose; if for no other reason, from being generally
carried out on the roads, fields, &c.—that is to say,
just where provocation and opportunity for conflicts
present themselves at every corner.   Nevertheless, it
has its own peculiar advantages, which should be
utilised.   The school method is much better adapted
for the correction of restiveness, because it affords more
direct and efficient means for acquiring perfect control
over the horse's movements.   It is, however, from a
judicious combination of the two systems that the
best results may be hoped for.   We shall, therefore,
give first a general sketch of the principles of both,
pointing out as we proceed how each may be best
applied for the object in view, as also for that of getting over difficulties with horses that are not restive.
We shall next lay down the outlines of a method
applicable in nearly all cases of insubordination; and,
finally, specify for some particular forms of restiveness
the treatment that promises the best results; as also
what should be avoided—for very much depends on
this.   In a word, we propose showing that a rational
methodical treatment of what is called vice offers much
better chances of success than violent measures : and
with this general statement of the aim and object of
this treatise we now conclude our introductory chapter.

# PART I.

# SEATS AND SADDLES

# CHAPTER I.

THE skeleton of the horse is a very wonderful and beautiful piece of mechanism, which no one who takes an interest in such matters can contemplate without experiencing the pleasurable feeling that perfect harmony of proportion always inspires. We were about to add, fitness and adaptability to our purposes, but remembered, just in proper time, that this would be, after all, a very incorrect mode of expression ; for, in truth, what is highly desirable is, that we should limit and adapt our requirements to the capabilities of this mechanism, and not simply to our own convenience, which but too frequently leads to abuse, as we shall now proceed to show.

The horse depicted in Plate I.* is of an average description, and stands in a natural position, its head and neck stretched forwards, and the hind legs, instead of being perfectly perpendicular from the hocks downwards, slightly brought forward to assist in maintaining the equilibrium. The animal is *at rest;* there is nothing constrained in its attitude; but the eye tells us at once that a somewhat greater proportion of its weight

* Taken from Seeger's 'System der Reitkunst.'

rests on the fore legs than on the hind ones, owing, as one sees, to the projecting position of the head and neck, which are much heavier than the tail at the other extremity.

Looking now at the spinal column, the framework of the back, on which the rider's weight is to be placed, we perceive that, whilst the under line of the vertebræ is nearly straight, although not quite horizontal, inclining somewhat downwards towards the forehand, the spinal processes of the first thirteen vertebræ of the back (dorsal vertebræ), reckoning from the point where the neck is attached, incline backwards, whereas those of the fifteenth, sixteenth, seventeenth, and eighteenth dorsal, and the six lumbar vertebræ, incline forwards; the fourteenth dorsal vertebra, with its process, standing perfectly upright, and forming, as it were, the keystone of the arch thus presented. It is very obvious that this inclination of the processes towards a central point is intended to and does limit the motion of the back downwards and upwards (*i. e.*, vertically), so that, in fact, this fourteenth dorsal vertebra becomes the *centre of motion of the horse's body*—the point about which the several movements of the fore and hind legs are performed with various degrees of rapidity, either simultaneously or successively, and which constitute the paces of the horse; and this is further shown by the distribution and points of attachment of the muscles of the back and adjacent parts of the fore and hind quarters. Putting, therefore, the progressive movement of the animal out of the question as being equally applicable to all its parts, the internal motion of the several parts of the body increases in proportion to their distance from the fourteenth vertebra; *and the*

*same is applicable to burdens placed on the horse's back,
especially a rider, whose frame is subject to its own
peculiar motions, some of which are caused by the progressive movement of the bearer.*

It has been already pointed out, that in consequence
of the projecting position of the head and neck, especially when the horse stands at ease, a somewhat
greater proportion of its total weight falls on the fore
legs than on the hinder ones ; and when it depresses
its head still more than is represented in Plate I.—for
instance, for the purpose of grazing—the animal puts
forward one fore leg, and usually at the same time the
hind leg of the opposite side, for the purpose of securing its equilibrium ; and even horses standing still,
especially under a load, do the same, in order to rest
each pair of legs alternately.

We learn two facts from this : first, that the fore
legs are essentially bearers, and that the hinder ones,
although chiefly propellers, are also to a certain extent
bearers ; and, secondly, that a perpendicular line falling
through the centre of gravity of a horse, as here represented, would lie nearer to the shoulder than the perpendicular E F, which falls through the centre of motion
—that is, the fourteenth dorsal vertebra—and would
probably cut the twelfth, or perhaps the eleventh, in
some horses.   Now, instead of going into the scientific
detail of centres of gravity, which might prove difficult
to some and tedious to most readers, we shall endeavour
to render intelligible all that is really important to be
known, by a very simple experiment that any one can
repeat for themselves.   *a b c d*, fig. 1, represents a
piece of thin board 9 inches long by 4 inches wide, at
whose corners four legs of about 7½ inches long are

fixed on with one screw each, so as to allow them
to be moved either to front or rear, but sufficiently
tight to retain them in the position in which they are
placed. A small weight is then placed exactly on the
centre point of the board at $p$, the four legs being ad-

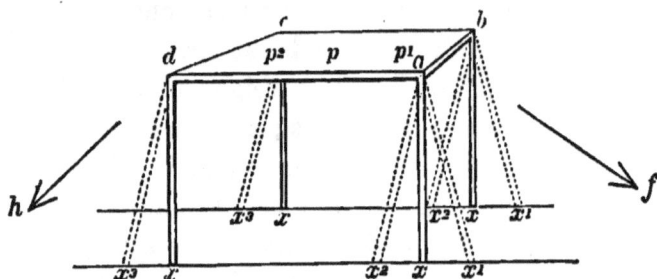

Fig. 1.

justed square, as at $x\ x\ x\ x$. If the weight be not
so heavy as to overcome the slight friction of the heads
of the screws, the board will remain in its position—
that is, it will stand; but if it be removed towards one
end of the board, say to $p^1$, it will cause the board to
turn on the screwheads, and, if not prevented, slide
down towards $f$; but if the two legs at this end be
bent backwards to $x^1\ x^1$, the board will support the
weight as before. In like manner, if the weight be
removed in the other direction to $p^2$, the legs being
square, the same thing will occur, and the board will
turn on its legs and slide down towards $h$, which, however may be prevented by adjusting the same pair of
legs as before, and which here represent the hind legs
of the horse, to the position $x^2\ x^2$, and in both these
cases the board will assume a slanting position, in which
the end $a\ b$ will be lower. Or, the weight being at
$p^2$, the board may be made to stand by adjusting the
*other pair* of legs, representing the horse's fore legs, to

the position $x^3$ $x^3$, and in this case it will slant the other way, the end $c$ $d$ being lower.

Now this is just what takes place when a rider is put on a horse's back in analogous positions, leaving out of the question for the moment the influence of the overhanging head and neck on the stability of the machine. Referring back to Plate I., we see, in fact, that the points $a$ and $d$ of the board correspond with the hip and shoulder joints A and D on the one side of the horse, as $b$ and $c$ do with the same joints on the other, and these are the two points of support of the back, whilst $p$ corresponds with the fourteenth vertebra at E; and, still leaving the head and neck out of the question, the rider placed here would sit not only *directly over the centre of motion, but also over the centre of gravity*—that is to say, a central point equally removed from each of its four supporting points;* he would occupy the apex or summit of a regular pyramid, the most stable of all forms of construction.

Let us now suppose the rider, or the weight, whatever it may consist of, placed farther back towards the horse's

* It is to be remarked that the points on which the horse's feet stand seldom coincide exactly—that is, lie precisely *under* the shoulder and hip joints respectively. The fore feet especially seldom reach, even with the toes, the perpendiculars from the shoulder-joints. With Eclipse they did so naturally, with tolerably well-built horses moderately " set up " they will generally do so ; and if the setting-up is carried beyond a certain point, they not only reach but project before them, the two hind feet either following proportionately in the same direction, or going to the rear, as may be seen when the horse-dealer "stretches a horse," in order to show how much ground it covers. There is a great difference, too, between the jointed flexible legs of a horse, and the rigid straight ones represented in fig. 1. An animal always exerts a certain amount of muscular action to maintain its balance even when resting.

loins, corresponding to the point $p^1$ of fig. 1. What
does the horse do, if compelled to stand still under a
burden that is more than his hind legs can easily support with perpendicular hocks? Let the reader turn
to Plate VII., where the English hussar there presented
shows the horse extending his hind legs precisely in
the way indicated in fig. 1, $x^1 x^1$. What between the
rider sitting at the hinder part of the saddle and the
weight of the enormous pack, the perpendicular passing through the centre of gravity of the whole falls considerably in rear of the fourteenth vertebra. This figure
is photographed from life, and is very instructive. The
horse, certainly not a fair specimen of the regiment or
of the cavalry in general, was selected, probably, for no
other reason than because he could be easily brought
to stand still during the operation ; and the clearness
of the lines of the original everywhere except about
the head, which he probably tossed once or twice,
shows that he did so, which was rendered possible, under the burden he had to bear, and the mode in which
it was placed on his back, *only* by this very position
of his hind legs ; he *could not* stand straight under it,
and the less so because his hind quarters are weaker in
proportion than the forehand. The position of the
head and neck has much to do with it, but this we
shall have to consider further on.

The cases in which a horse, when standing still, and
weighted *chiefly* on his forehand, assumes with his fore
legs the positions indicated in fig. 1 by $x^3 x^3$ or $x^2 x^2$,
occur so frequently that it is quite superfluous to
devote a figure to their illustration. Put a man on a
horse without a saddle, and with nothing but a halter
on the animal's head, and he will inevitably slip for-

wards till his seat comes in contact with the withers. Let him then stand still, and the horse, especially if a young or untrained one, will most probably shove forward his hind or fore legs in one of those two ways.

There remains a third case for consideration—namely, where the horse, being weighted back to the line G H, Plate I., brings his hind legs under him up to the line I K, *but with the hocks bent.* This is the position into which manege-horses have to be brought for certain definite purposes, the general object being to enable them to make short turns on the hind quarters or croup, the forehand turning round this latter; whereas, with a horse weighted on the centre line E F, Plate I., the hind and fore quarters both turn equally round a common point, and with one weighted principally on the forehand, the hind quarters will turn round the former.

Now, in order to avoid drawing false conclusions from these facts, we must take another view of the question. What we have hitherto inquired into is, the effect of certain modes of distributing the weight on a horse's back when in a state of rest on the position of his legs with regard to that weight; but the really important thing to know is, how these various modes influence the horse's action. It was, however, necessary to enter into the preliminary inquiry, because most of the conditions governing a horse's attitude in a state of rest continue to be equally imperative after action has commenced, and some even more so; for it is more dangerous to the horse to lose his balance when in motion, especially at high degrees of speed, than when standing still.

We may put the questions to be resolved as follows: 1st, How does the distribution of the weight to be carried affect the horse's speed? and, 2dly, How does action affect equilibrium or balance?

The way in which these questions present themselves points directly to their solution; and, as regards the first, it is to the horse's legs, and the mode in which they are *moved*, that we must look, just as in the former case we looked to the mode in which they are *fixed*. There is, however, a great difference observable between the functions of the hind and fore legs when we come to compare action with rest. In the latter, we were justified in looking on both pairs *equally* as bearers; in the former, the fore legs are still employed *chiefly* as bearers, and only in a smaller degree as propellers, whereas the hind legs act *chiefly* as propellers and in a less degree as bearers. It should follow from this, that we may favour the propelling power of the hind legs by weighting forward within *certain limits;* and this we know to be the case—the long stride of the race-horse *is* favoured by the well-known forward seat of the jockey. Well, what are the limits? In the case of the jockey it is difficult to draw a "hard and fast" line, because his total weight is inconsiderable, and the distances to be got over are inconsiderable; and this is precisely the reason why heavier riders, especially when they have to do long distances, should not ride forward like the jockey, because they are sure, sooner or later, to use up their horses' fore legs by making them exclusively bearers : even race-horses will break down under the light weight, and some jocks are unfortunate in this respect.

And if this be true, it is equally so that placing the weight too near the hind legs must diminish their propelling power, by converting them, in a greater degree, into bearers; and this may be done in two different ways, one of which, having a very definite object, is good in its way, whilst the other is, to say the least, of very questionable utility under any circumstances. The manege or school rider educates his horse to bear an increased proportion of the weight on its hind legs, these latter being brought forward *under the animal* with bent hocks; but his object not being speed—and it is well known that manege - training diminishes speed, for which reason, precisely, English riders scoff at the *haute école*, somewhat unadvisedly perhaps—the manege-rider is perfectly justified in acting as he does in order to attain other objects. It is, moreover, important to remark that if a horse's hind quarters be not sufficiently strong and pliable to enable them to endure the increased demand for bearing without annihilating their propelling power, such a horse will be incapable of high training in this sense.

The English hussar-horse in Plate VII. is precisely in this position, and having poor hind quarters, incapable of sustaining the weight thrown on them even with perpendicular hocks, much less with his legs bent under him like a school - horse, he is compelled to stretch them out like the props $x^1$ $x^1$ in fig. 1, and is therefore, even in a state of rest, more than half-way to the utmost reach of his stride; for the whole concern must roll over if he attempted, in galloping, to bring up these legs to the hoof-marks of the fore legs. There can be no question, therefore, but that weighting in this manner diminishes speed.*

Before going on to the second question, one word

* There is a justification for this kind of riding when the fore legs are groggy and the hind ones still good; and this expedient is of

more about the fore legs, which are, as has been said,
essentially bearers ; they are, however, to a certain
extent propellers, and must, at all events should, exercise a springy lever action, lifting the horse's body so
as to enable the propellers to shove it forwards.   Now,
neither the propulsive nor lifting action of the fore legs
can be properly exercised unless their several component levers (bones) form certain angles with each
other, and enable the hoof to touch the ground lightly,
and ready for a renewal of the action.  The fore foot
should be placed on the ground as one places the
palm of his hand on a table ; if the leg come down
straight and stiff, end on, like the props $x^3$ $x^3$ of fig. 1
—which may be as readily caused by a rider sitting too
far back on his horse, and being thrown by the action
of the hind quarter, with stiffened knees, into a stirrup
that is hung far forward in the saddle, as by one that,
sitting originally far forwards, comes down with a heavy
thud directly on the horse's withers—the fore legs must
suffer.   They are not so constructed as to be thrust
against the ground, end on like a pole, with impunity;
and if either of these forms of riding be carried to an
extreme, it prevents these legs from lifting the forehand in proper time or sufficiently; and the propellers
acting meanwhile, down comes the poor brute on his
head, and alas for the knees!  Sooner or later horses
are educated into stumbling in this way, the fore legs
being by degrees deprived of their elasticity.

And now as to the question of the mode in which
action affects equilibrium or balance.   The first point
to be observed is, that in walking and trotting the

adopted, especially by that class of riders who sit far back and still
manage to ruin their horses' fore legs, of which more anon.

horse moves its diagonal legs simultaneously, or nearly so—that is to say, the off fore and the near hind leg move together and alternate in this action with the near fore and off hind ones ; so that, whilst the one pair is being moved forwards the other sustains the weight of the animal ; and supposing the horse to be in equilibrio or balance, we might be led to suppose that the perpendicular line passing through the centre of gravity would fall exactly in the centre of a line connecting the fore and hind foot that remains on the ground. But this is not the case, except for the moment at which the movement is half completed.* Fig. 2, *A*, will make this more intelligible. The full

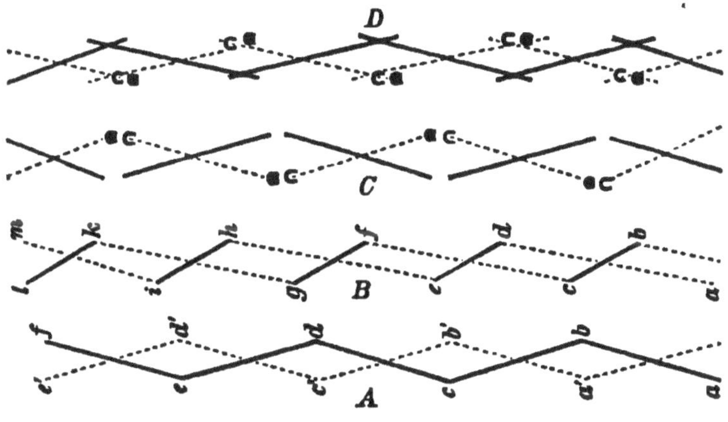

Fig. 2.

lines connect the pairs of feet as they alternately support the horse, whilst the dotted ones represent the

---

* In the manege movement called *piaffé*, in which the horse moves his limbs as in trotting but without gaining ground, the perpendicular in question does, in the alternate movement, always bisect the line connecting the two feet which are on the ground.

connection of those in motion. When it comes to the turn of the near hind foot at $a$, and the off fore one at $b$, to move up to their next position at $c$ $d$, the line $a$ $b$ becomes a dotted one, $a^1$ $b^1$, from the moment this pair of legs leaves the ground, the near fore and off hind legs at $c$ and $b$ becoming the supporters ; and so on alternately. But the dotted lines, in coming up successively to the position of the full ones, intersect the latter at *various* points of their length : the diagram shows them at the moment each successive step is *half* completed, the intersection of the two showing where the perpendicular from the centre of gravity falls. And this intersection—consequently, too, the weight to be supported—is always travelling *towards the fore leg that happens to be on the ground, and therefore the centre of gravity vibrates alternately from right to left, and* vice versa, *in trotting and walking.*

In cantering and galloping the case is different : the two legs at *the same side* are advanced simultaneously, the other two remaining behind. Still, supposing the animal to be in equilibrium, we observe the following to occur (see fig. 2, $B$) : the horse " leads " here with the two off feet—that is, canters on the right hand, the two near ones remaining behind *so long as he remains on this hand;* there is, therefore, not the same alternate vibration of the centre of gravity from right to left, and *vice versa*, as in trotting and walking, for it is always the same pair of feet, moreover, just as in trotting the diagonal ones, that mainly support the weight. In the diagram we see that the off hind and near fore legs, connected by the full lines, are both placed close under the centre of gravity in the succession of bounds, as shown at $b$ $c$, $d$ $e$, $f$ $g$,

&c., and act *chiefly* as bearers; whilst the near hind leg, *a*, acts *chiefly* as·a propeller, and the off fore leg, *d*, as a lifter, these two being connected by dotted lines in the successive bounds, *e h, g k*, &c., and the intersections of these full and dotted lines remain invariable.

This will serve to explain why it is that, although a *moderate* trot is less fatiguing to horses than any other pace for a long journey, on account of the pairs of legs being used as bearers and propellers *alternately*, some horses will, under the rider, break into a canter, the alternate shifting of their own and his weight from right to left becoming more fatiguing than the constant use of each pair of legs for the same functions; and the proof is, that many of these horses will go a steady trot in harness when they have only their own weight to adjust.  It also explains why horses, when *hurried* in their trot, and over-weighted in the forehand, whereby the bearers (fore legs) become unable to support the weight thrown more and more rapidly on them by the hind legs, which now act solely as propellers, naturally, and to save themselves from falling, "lead" with a fore leg, immediately followed by a hind one—that is to say, break into a canter, which gives them, instead of the alternate *lines* of support, *a b, b c, c d* (*A*, fig. 2), a permanent triangle, *k l m* (*B*, fig. 2), as a basis.

It may be objected that some horses will trot under the rider that will not do so in harness; no doubt this is because that rider knows how to adjust his weight to the peculiar exigencies of the horse; some, from various causes, being assisted in trotting by the rider's weight being adjusted in a particular way, of which a very remarkable instance is adduced in a footnote,

p. 52, of that very admirable work, 'The Handy Horse-Book.' There was some defect of the animal's construction in this case, that required the weight to be adjusted in a peculiar way : the halter and the riding barebacked tells the tale.

For the sake of simplicity, we have hitherto proceeded on the supposition that each of the two diagonal legs (of every pair) is lifted and set down simultaneously. This is not the case. One hears distinctly four beats in the case of walking and trotting ; and two, three, or four in cantering and galloping, according as the horse's weight is adjusted in the latter movements. Of the two legs acting in concert, the fore one is lifted and set down somewhat sooner than the hind one ; were this not the case, a horse could never tread in his own hoof-marks, much less beyond them, as we shall presently show to be the case. A musician could easily express on paper, by the appropriate notes, the cadence not only of each particular pace, but for each individual horse ;* and good judges are well aware that irregularity of beat points out something amiss in one or more legs. The ear often conveys to us valuable impressions on this very point that totally escape the eye even of the most practised. We all have heard of blind men being good judges of horse-flesh.†

Having now seen the effect of action on equilibrium, where such exists, it is necessary to point out its effects and consequences in cases where it does *not* exist. In

* In the 'Sonnambula,' Bellini has imitated very successfully the beat of several post-horses trotting and galloping just before Rudolfo enters on the scene.

† The theory of equilibrium, as set forth above, is not affected in the slightest degree by this want of perfect coincidence in the movement of the legs.

the diagrams *A*, *B*, fig. 2, the horse is made to tread with the hind foot *into* the track of the fore one (this is, in fact, a consequence of equilibrium); but we see very many horses bring their hind feet (in all paces) more or less ahead of the track or print of the fore ones ; indeed almost all young and untrained horses will do so, and, moreover, many whose work requires them to act thus—as, for instance, race-horses. This is best seen by the hoof-marks left on moist ground or sand, which will be found in double pairs instead of single ones after such horses. Now of course it would be as absurd to suppose that, under such circumstances, a horse takes shorter steps with his fore legs than with the hind ones, as to ignore what the immortal Hudibras pointed out long ago—namely, that when, having but one spur, you make one side of your horse to get along, the other is sure to follow ; a fact well known to Irish " bull-riders " at Ballinasloe.

There is another class of horses that, instead of overstepping, come short of the track of the fore feet with the hind ones, and almost all horses do this at starting —in fact they cannot do otherwise ; these, too, leave a double track.

Now those that overstep will be usually found to be such as are over-weighted on the forehand, whilst those that step short are usually such as are over-weighted behind, without the hind legs being brought under the weight in a bent position like the manege-horse, or that have some weakness, want of due proportion or other deficiency, in their hind quarters.

When a horse oversteps with his hind legs the track of the fore feet (*C*, fig. 2,) the succession of full lines connecting the two diagonal feet in each alternate movement is not, as shown in *A*, continuous, but broken ; there is, therefore, an interval of time during which the weight of the horse (and rider) is not supported diagonally in the usual manner, but vibrates, as it were, from one fixed basis to a more forward one. The animal is off the ground with all four legs for a moment in rapid trotting, for instance—the consequence is, that there must be *less stability ;* and we know from experience that, when this is carried to a great extent, the horse " over-reaches," as it is called, and comes down ; but, on the other hand, the advantage is gained of getting over the ground more rapidly; for on comparing *C* with *A*, it is evident that more ground has been covered in the former than in the latter with the same number of strides, which are therefore longer. The advantage conferred by throwing the weight forward is, therefore, that it tends to increase the speed; the disadvantages attendant on it are, diminished stability, and the rapid using up of the fore legs, for it is on these alternately that the whole weight pivots, as it were, during the moments of vibration from each fixed basis to the succeeding one, as explained above.

When a horse steps short—that is to say, does not attain to the track of the fore feet with the hinder ones (*D*, fig. 2)—the exact contrary of the above takes place ; the full lines connecting the diagonal feet overlap each other constantly—the animal covers part of the same ground twice in its successive strides ; these, therefore, are shorter, and it requires a greater number of them to cover a given space. On the other hand, the stability is more perfect, but the hind legs are unduly converted into bearers, and suffer in consequence. That they really are so is shown by the fact of the short stepping

taking place.   They cannot act sufficiently as propellers.*   What is said here applies equally to canter or
gallop as to trot.   It has been pointed out above that,
in the case of the horse covering its own footsteps
exactly, and leaving only a single track, the fore legs
are always lifted somewhat sooner than the hind ones,
and not exactly simultaneously with them, which produces, as we have seen, the cadence peculiar to each
pace, audible to the ear.   If the beat be regular, and,
the ground remaining the same, the intensity of the
sound alike for each footstep, the presumption is that
all four legs are equally good ; but if one tread be
heavy and another light, we may take it for granted
that there is something amiss with the foot or leg that
makes the latter.   With horses, however, that either
overstep or tread short (*C* and *D*, fig. 2), the case is
different; we hear constantly *two stronger and two
weaker beats*, supposing the legs and feet to be sound.
The former—stronger ones—will be found to proceed, if
we pay attention, from the fore legs in the horse that
oversteps,—the two hind ones, chiefly used as propellers, "dinting" into the ground with the toes ; with the
short stepper, on the contrary, we perceive that they
proceed from the hind legs, which are stamped down;
and if one leg be defective, we hear, in such cases, three
different degrees of intensity of sound, which vary according to the leg and the mode of action.†

* Horses that at first naturally overstep will, after a certain
amount of work, come to step short ; the fore legs having suffered,
they ease them by throwing the weight on the hind ones.

† Dishonest dealers are well aware of this, and, to cover it, will
sometimes make a horse temporarily lame on one foot to conceal
a permanent defect of the corresponding one; the horse will then
tread "gingerly " on that pair.

We must now remind the reader that we have, up to this point, taken no account of the influence exercised by the overhanging weight of the horse's head and neck on the animal's equilibrium, having proceeded altogether on the supposition of this being analogous to that of the little instrument represented in fig. 1. It has been shown, however, that the centre of motion,—that is to say, the point round which all other parts of the animal move when in action—or, what comes to the same thing, the point where the least motion is felt, —is situated somewhere in a perpendicular falling through the fourteenth dorsal vertebra, Plate I.; and it has been intimated that the perpendicular through the centre of gravity of a horse naturally falls through some one or other of the vertebræ from the tenth to the thirteenth, that are situate nearer to the neck. A horse can *go* with these two centres in the relative position described here. It favours certain special purposes—as, for instance, racing, and perhaps riding to hounds, to a certain extent—just as it suits the purpose of the manege-rider to bring the centre of gravity further back towards the loins than the fourteenth vertebra; but for *all general purposes* it is of the greatest importance that the two perpendiculars passing respectively through these two centres should be made to coincide,—and this is the aim and object of all school-riding, except for the *haut manège.* Above all, it is indispensable for military purposes.

In fact, in racing, and to a certain extent in hunting, a horse is not required to move otherwise than in nearly straight lines or gentle curves. A jockey that understands the work will ride differently in the latter and the former, and will immediately change his seat when he comes "into the straight." *    On the contrary, the manege-rider requires very short deliberate turns at *low* degrees of speed, and attains his object as above described; but for general riding it is of great importance—for the cavalry, indispensable—to be able to turn in sharp curves at *higher* degrees of speed.

Instead of instituting a mathematical and physical inquiry into the advantages of making the centres of gravity and motion coincide, let us take from everyday life one or two instances that illustrate the principle very satisfactorily.    In a common two-wheeled cart the whole body of the machine turns round on the axle, and the centre of motion lies in a perpendicular falling through the mid-point of this.    A carter that understands his business always adjusts the load in such a manner that it neither presses too much on the horse's back by lying too far forward, nor on his neck by being too far back in the cart—in fact he makes the centres of motion and gravity to correspond as nearly as possible, knowing from experience that his horse *draws* the cart with greater ease, and *can turn* corners, &c., more readily, when the load is thus adjusted, than in any other manner.    For special purposes, as going up hill, he shifts the weight forward, but he is cautious in turning the horse when the load is on the back: there is always danger of falling.    Sometimes, when his object is to turn the cart round sharply on its own ground, he shifts the weight to the rear, *the horse* having then perfect liberty to circle round in the required direction; but he never adopts this for a journey, be it ever so short.

* The speed of race-horses is notoriously different on straight and circular courses.    The absolutely speedier horse does not always come first to the post on the latter.

Again, in a ship or boat of any kind, people that have experienced sea-sickness soon find out where the centre of motion lies, and nestle round it; and the master who sails her knows well that his cargo or load, whatever it may be, must be so stowed away that the centre of gravity of the whole coincides with the centre of motion of the vessel. This is what is called "trim," as we all know; and the yachtsman knows well the effect of sending a man or two into the bows, when running before the wind, and the use of keeping his hands aft when in stays; but he will be chary of altering the builder's trim, which makes these two centres coincide mathematically; he may never find it again, as has happened in some remarkable instances. Now the horse under a rider must have the trim that suits the objects of the latter; and for general purposes the ship-builder's trim or the carter's trim will be found the most advantageous. The bringing the rider's body, from the hips upwards, slightly forwards or backwards, will answer exactly the same purposes as the shifting the hands in a yacht or the sacks in a cart. It can answer no good purpose to alter the regular trim. To persist in sailing a boat out of trim ends in a capsize, or in carrying away spars at least; just as riding out of trim usually terminates in a "purl," and always in the premature destruction of the horse's legs.

And just as too heavy a bowsprit or jib-boom will destroy the trim of a boat, the overhanging position of the horse's head and neck destroys the animal's proper trim *after a rider is placed on its back;* and the question is, therefore, how this may be remedied, seeing that we cannot shift a head and neck like a jib-boom. Fig. 3 shows three levers, $d\,N$, $d\,O$, $d\,P$, of equal

length, all moving round the same common centre or
prop *d*, which corresponds to the junction of the ver-

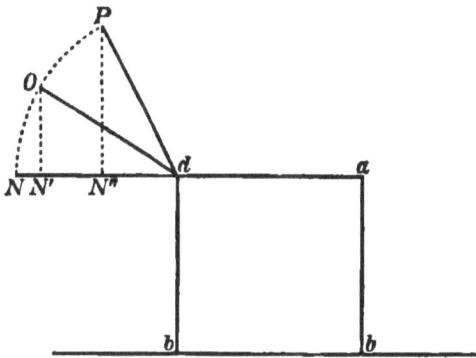

Fig. 3.

tebræ of the neck with those of the back in the horse.
Now the longer the lever the greater its power—that
is to say, a given weight will act more powerfully at
the extremity of a long lever than of a short one, in
the exact proportion of their relative lengths.   The
true expression is, however, that a given weight acting
on a lever of this kind exercises a downward (perpendicular) pressure in direct proportion to the distance
at which the perpendicular from (or through) it falls
from the prop.   Therefore, if the head and neck, *d N*,
be stretched out horizontally, the relative weight is ·
represented by the whole amount by which the point
*N* lies outside of the basis *b b*; and if the head and
neck be lifted to the position *d O*, it will be represented by the shorter distance *d N'*; and if still more
elevated to *d P*, then by the still shorter one *d N"*.
Consequently, the relative overhanging weight of those
portions of the horse's body may be diminished in proportion as their position is brought nearer to that re-

presented by $d\,P$ in the figure; and the further effect
of this is, that the centre of gravity of the whole
machine resting on the basis $b\,b$, is thrown farther
back on the line $d\,a$. A horse's neck is not, however,
an inflexible straight line like an ordinary lever.
Moreover, the head, which forms no inconsiderable
portion of the overhanging weight, can be bent at
various angles to the neck. We have it therefore in
our power not only to diminish the external prepon-
derance of these members by altering their relative
position as described above, but also actually to diminish the distance at which the perpendicular falls outside the basis—first, by bending the neck, by which
the length of the lever is curtailed; and still further,
by making the head assume more and more acute—
that is, smaller—angles with the line of the neck,
whether this latter be straight or curved.

This is shown by fig. 4, where the natural—that is,
unimproved—position of the head and neck makes the
perpendicular fall at the distance $D\,N$ outside the
basis of the animal; and this corresponds nearly to a
line of gravity, $x\,y$, falling through one of the dorsal
vertebræ nearer to the neck than the fourteenth, to
which reference has been made. And by elevating the
neck somewhat, curving it at the same time, and making
the head assume an acuter angle with it, we bring back
the centre of gravity perhaps to $E\,F$, the perpendicular
falling through the fourteenth vertebra, or centre of motion—and this is the safest and most generally applicable position: for cavalry purposes it is absolutely
indispensable. Finally, if we bring the neck still higher
up, curving it still more, as shown in the figure, we
can bring the centre of gravity back to the line $G\,H$,

as the manege-rider does ; who, however, at the same time, gets the toes of the horse's hind feet up to the

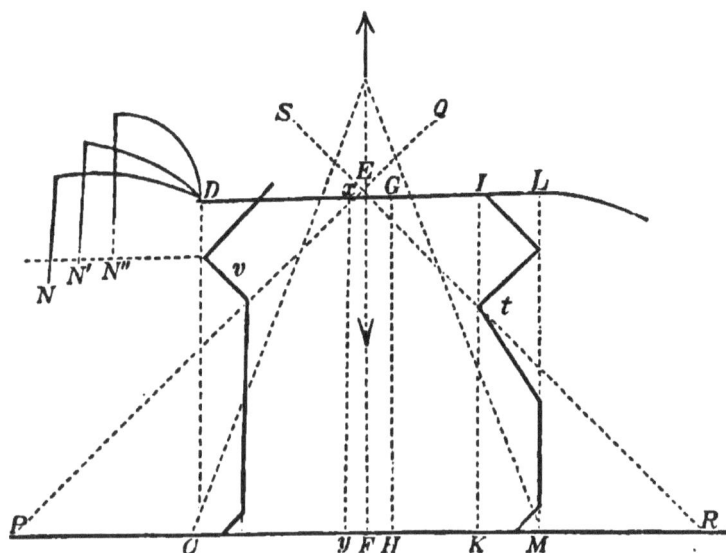

Fig. 4.

line *I K* in a bent position, which naturally brings the croup down* (see fig. 1, $x^2$ $x^2$).

This same figure taken together with Plate II. brings us to the final result at which we have aimed all through this chapter—namely, the equilibrium of the horse in motion as compared with the same in a state of rest. Under the latter supposition (rest), we could only show, from the formation of the spinal column (back), that the fourteenth vertebra indicates, by its

* It is necessary to remark that in this case the basis of the figure remains as before at *C* and *M*, the hind legs acting not merely as mechanical props, but maintaining a portion of the weight by mus-cular action, which, however, must not be too long continued.

peculiar shape and position, a different function from
that of the other vertebræ, all of which evidently admit of movement towards it, within certain limits,
whilst this one, not being adapted for this purpose, may
so far be considered to be intended for the centre of
motion.   But the construction of the horse's legs, and
the relative position of the various bones composing
them, furnish us with very clear proof of this same
vertebra being the real centre of motion when the
horse is in action.   For there is one bone in each of
the hind and fore legs through which the remainder of
the limb acts as a lever on the whole frame, either for
the purpose of propelling it (hind legs), or supporting
and lifting it (fore legs).   These are the thigh-bone *t*,
and the arm-bone *v* (fig. 4), whose upper ends have
their fulcrums or points of support in the hip-bones A
and shoulder-blades D (Plate I.) respectively, the power
being applied through the medium of the remaining
portions of the legs at their lower ends.   Now the
greatest *result* of lever action is exercised at a right
angle to the lever, and drawing the lines *P Q* and *R S*
through the lower ends of these two bones *at right
angles to them, we find that they intersect* (or cross)
*each other precisely at this same fourteenth vertebra.*
The figure shows us, indeed, the horse in a state of rest,
and not in action; but it is necessary to remember that
the propelling action of the hind leg *commences, and is
precisely most powerful,* when the thigh-bone is in this
position, diminishing in intensity as the leg is stretched
out towards *R*, and the angles become *flatter;* whereas,
on the contrary, the supporting and lifting action of
the fore leg *ends*, the arm-bone being as shown in the
figure, and is also most intense, diminishing as the fore

PLATE II.

THE MUSCLES OF THE MACHINE.

leg is stretched out towards $P$, and the angles become flatter. It is therefore evident that, *both in a state of rest and of action, the fourteenth vertebra is constantly the centre of motion;* and it is precisely from our practical knowledge of this beautiful mechanism that judges of horses attach so much importance to the length of these two levers, and to their lying at right angles to the hip-bone and shoulder-blade respectively —which is recognised by the form of the haunch, and what we call a good shoulder; the length of the stride and its power depending, as is very evident, on those particulars to a great extent.

A farther proof of the same fact may be gathered from Plate II., which shows the principle muscles, and the way in which they are arranged. It is those in the back, loins, hips, and shoulders, that concern us here more especially; and we perceive that the principal ones of these all coalesce, as it were, into the large flat tendon covering the identical portion of the back pointed out as the centre of motion. This tendon, like all others, is devoid of contractile power; and the corresponding sets of muscles of the fore and back hand exert *their* contractile powers upon it in opposite directions, whilst it remains stationary, so to say—the whole process having a certain analogy with the familiar instance of a pair of curtains drawn forward by cords to the middle of a window.

According to the laws of mechanics, when two forces of equal intensity cross each other, as the lines $P\ Q$, $R\ S$, do in fig. 4, the line in which the combined result of both is further propagated will lie equally distant from and between the two original forces—and this is, in the instance before us, perpendicularly upwards, as shown by the upper arrow; and the antagonistic force of gravitation — in plain language, the weight of the rider—*will be best met* when it acts in precisely the opposite direction, or perpendicularly downwards in the direction of the lower arrow; and therefore, if the weight of the rider lie, from his mode of sitting, across this perpendicular—for instance, towards the shoulders —the force coming *from* this direction will be met more directly and consumed in proportion, that coming from the other being *spared*.

The two forces of the hind and fore legs may not be, however, and in many horses, in consequence of want of symmetry, are not, equal in intensity. In untrained horses they seldom are. Judicious handling and riding are nothing else, in fact, than finding a proper balance of forces, as well for the untrained well-built horse as for one that is defective in symmetry.

It would carry us too far to go into the detail of the various modes in which the forces exerted by pairs of the hind and fore legs respectively cross each other— as also the centre of gravity itself in walk, trot, canter, &c. The proper methods of shifting the rider's weight from right to left, so as to favour the diagonal action of the pairs of feet, may be easily deduced from the study of these. But it is not our object to write a treatise on equitation; and for intelligent riders, what has been already said will suffice to clear up the doubts that may arise in practice. Indeed the scope of the whole of this chapter has been to set men thinking for themselves, instead of working by rule of thumb, and not to dictate any particular method to them.

# CHAPTER II.

IF it were merely a question of riding bare-backed, we might at once go on to apply the principles of equilibrium of the horse in motion, as developed in the foregoing chapter, to the various kinds of seats. It would be only reasonable, one should suppose, to accommodate our saddles to our seats, just as we do every other instrument to the purposes for which it is intended; but this is precisely what is very seldom done, and in the great majority of instances the rider sits his horse just in the fashion his saddle allows, or perhaps compels, him to do. Three-fourths of the time and trouble that are devoted in military riding-schools in endeavouring to get the men to sit in a uniform manner might be spared, and the desired result much more certainly attained, by properly adjusting the saddle to the horse *and* man, instead of forcing the latter into a contest with a mechanical difficulty that requires a constant exertion of muscular power; and this latter, being limited in extent and duration, is sure to succumb in the contest, leaving the horse's back to bear the punishment. It is therefore a matter of some importance to understand clearly the mechanical principles applicable to this piece of horse furniture, as it will enable every rider to ascertain exactly what he wants, and how to attain his object, whatever that may be—as also to save his horse's back, and his own purse, and perhaps neck.

To begin with the under surface of the saddle—the portion coming in contact with the horse's back—we find two principal points for consideration,—its shape or form, and its size or extent. One general mechanical principle applies to both—namely, that the larger the surface over which a given amount of pressure is equably spread or divided, the less will be the action on any given point of the other surface in contact; and this translated into plain English means, as *regards shape*, that the under surface of the saddle should bear as nearly as possible the same relation to that part of the horse's back it is intended to occupy, as a mould does to the cast that is taken from it, always saving and excepting that strip lying over the horse's backbone, which must remain altogether *out* of contact. The notion of making one portion come into closer contact than another, "giving a gripe," with the intention of preventing the saddle slipping, is altogether erroneous, because it is the *sum total* of the pressure which produces the cohesion between two surfaces; its being concentrated on one point or line does not increase this amount, but is very likely to make a hole in the horse's back. Which part of the horse's back it should be fitted to has been " dimly shadowed forth" in Chapter I., but shall be more clearly and accurately determined in the course of this present one.

As regards size or extent of surface the meaning is, that the greater this is with a *given* weight, the less will be the pressure on any given point, and consequently the less risk of sore back, *provided always that the pressure be equably distributed over the whole surface.* To make a saddle a yard long, and put the weight altogether at one of its extremities, is not the way to attain this very desirable object, as shall be more fully explained presently.*

There must, however, be some limit to the size of a saddle, for its own absolute weight is a matter of serious consideration : it goes into the scale with the jock. *Let the size be proportioned to the weight to be carried,* and if you have a tender-backed horse, make it a little bigger than would be otherwise necessary. Of course a jock can ride his race on a thing that is more a contrivance for hanging up a pair of stirrups than a saddle, whilst a sixteen-stone rider must divide his weight over as large a surface as convenient.

There are two ways in which the weight of the saddle may be decreased without its useful *under* surface being narrowed. The first is to avoid extending the frame (tree), or indeed any other part of the saddle, beyond the surfaces where it really has to support pressure ; and this being exercised *chiefly* in a perpendicular direction, it is not only useless but absurd to make these extend *too* far down over the ribs laterally. The second is to use, for the tree, materials combining great strength and moderate elasticity, with the least possible weight. A civilian saddle, made altogether of wood, is a very clumsy affair, and it is therefore the

---

* As familiar illustrations of the principle may be mentioned the difference of depth of track of broad and narrow tired wheels, or of a roller as compared with both : or, a board of one foot square will sink deeper into soft ground under a man's weight; than one of double that size ; and this latter will sink as deep as the former if weighted *only* at one end.

practice to reduce the volume of the wood, and regain
the strength thus sacrificed by iron platings.  This
metal is, however, very inelastic : if the plates be made
thin and light, they bend, and thus retain the wood in
a distorted shape ; if thick, they are heavy, and very
liable to break with a severe shock, or, if not, to convey this rudely to the horse's shoulder or back, instead of acting as the buffer does between two railway
trucks.  The platings should be made of steel, not too
highly tempered, and it ought to be possible to devise
means of strengthening the wood of that part of the
tree we allude to without increasing its bulk, and
with a diminution of its weight.  As to military saddles, they are best made wholly of wood and without
any iron whatever.  The necessity of attaching a pack
makes the question of neat appearance altogether
secondary, and the weight that must be carried renders it imperative to economise every ounce that is
possible.  Moreover, once introduce iron into the com-
position of a saddle and you must have a smith and a
forge to enable you to repair a broken one, which is
often out of the question in the field.  The original
Hungarian saddle had not a particle of iron on it ; no
doubt it was subject to breakage, but it could be re-
paired or a new one made at the side of a ditch, and in
time for the next day's march.  We nineteenth-century
men have improved it everywhere, especially in England, up to more than double its original weight, to a
nearly total incapacity for repair or alteration, and to
being the most efficient instrument conceivable for
making holes in horses' backs.

Supposing, now, the under surface of the saddle to
have the proper form and size, the next point to be

determined is, where to put the weight. As we cannot, in consequence of this being a man, divide and spread it out *equably* over the whole upper part of the saddle as we would inert matter of any kind, we must place the rider's *centre* of gravity exactly over the centre of the bearing surface of the saddle, for this is the only single *point* which, being loaded, transmits the pressure equably to the rest of the surface. Take a small common table, and place it exactly level on sand, grass, or soft ground, then put a weight precisely in the centre of the table, and measure the depth to which the feet had been forced into the soil—you will find it to be the same for all four feet, if the surface on which the table stands be equally soft throughout ; then shift the table a few inches, having previously removed the weight, and place this near one of the ends instead of in the middle,—measure again and you will find that the pair of legs nearest to the weight have penetrated much deeper than the others ; therefore, in order to equalise the pressure, the rider's weight should be placed in the centre of the saddle.

But this is not all. Place a piece of stout board about two feet long on the ground, stand on one end of it, and you will find that the other loses its contact with the ground, and is more or less tilted up into the air—the board has become a lever. Now, make a motion as if about to jump, but without quitting your position on the board ; this latter will, being out of contact with the ground at the further end, be shoved onwards in that direction. This is precisely what happens when a rider sits at one end of the saddle, generally the hinder one : this one is pressed down into the horse's back, the other, generally the front end,

D

is tilted up, and at every movement of the horse and rider the whole saddle is shoved forward till stopped by the withers, which it will probably wound ; and then it is either the groom's, or the saddler's, or the horse's fault, and the saddle is thrown aside and some new patent contrivance adopted, which of course does not remedy a defect that depends on the rider himself.

We may now go a step further. Suppose the saddle be placed with its centre exactly over the combined centres of gravity and motion (line $E\ F$, fig. 4), and the rider in the centre of the saddle, there will be, first, an equable distribution of the combined weight of horse *and* rider on all four legs, both in a state of rest and action ; secondly, the movements of the horse, centring in this point, have the least possible tendency to disturb the seat of the rider or the position of the saddle ; thirdly, the weight of the rider being equably distributed over the whole surface of the saddle in contact with the horse's back, is therefore less likely to injure any one portion of this ; nor does it convert the saddle into a lever, and shove it forwards or backwards.   Again, let us suppose the saddle as before, but the rider sitting altogether at its hinder end for instance, and there will be, first, the horse's equilibrium destroyed ; secondly, the rider himself, being nearer to the hind legs, will first receive an impulse from the direction $R\ S$, and be thrown forward till he meets that coming from the direction $P\ Q$, and these two forces, instead of resolving each other from one common point into their sum total, neutralise each other partially in successive shocks at the expense of the horse's legs.   It will be said that the use of the stirrups is to prevent the rider being thus thrown forward. No doubt they do, and this kind of rider always sticks out his legs towards the horse's shoulder on the line $Q\ P$; in other words, *he transmits the shock from the hind legs to the fore ones* through the medium of the stirrups (this, by the way, is the reason why stirrup-leathers are broken), of course shoving the saddle constantly forward, and these men's girths can never be drawn tight enough to prevent the saddle tilting up in front. Thirdly, of course his weight is not distributed equably over the whole under surface of the saddle. This is the man that manufactures sit-fasts, or, at the very least, transforms his horse's back from its natural colour into a strange pattern of white and grey blotches.

Some men would find it inconvenient to sit otherwise than well back in their saddles, and some kinds of riding *seem* to be more easily done in this form than in any other. Now it is evident enough from the foregoing, that if the part of the saddle occupied by the rider be placed over the line $E\ F$, fig. 4, the horse's balance is not necessarily deranged or the centre of motion interfered with so long as the rider keeps this position; but there always remains the difficulty about the unequal distribution of the weight, and the saddle slipping. Most English gentlemen ride more or less in this fashion, and, from our way of rising in the stirrups whilst trotting, are constantly transferring their weight from one end of the saddle to the other. Of course the horse's balance is thereby subjected to constant changes, and not unfrequently a misunderstanding between horse and rider ensues, terminating in a disaster: but we must not anticipate.

There is another consideration of great importance

with regard to the place of the saddle—namely, that it should interfere the least possible with the action of the muscles of the horse's fore and back hand. Looking at Plate II., we see the back covered with a broad tendon, into which, as has been already pointed out, the muscles of these two parts are inserted, and on which their contractile action is exercised. The saddle should not extend much, if at all, beyond the limits of this flat tendon, because, by doing so, it will be sure to impede more or less the free action of the muscles, whereas the tendon is rather assisted than impeded in its functions by a weight being placed on it; and it is also evident that a rider sitting at one end of his saddle instead of in the centre, will produce the same injurious effect.

The next question to be determined is, To what part of the saddle should the girths be attached? Now it is very evident that, if the placing of the weight in the centre of the saddle has the effect of transmitting an equal amount of pressure to all that part of the horse's back with which the latter is in contact, the attaching the girths so as to act *directly* on the centre of the saddle will have precisely the same effect; and the *friction* that results—that is, the adhesiveness produced by pressure—will be equable throughout, and of course least likely to injure any one particular point. It was a very prevalent idea some years ago, that " the point-strap "—that is to say, the girth that was placed well forward in the saddle—was the thing to depend on to prevent the saddle slipping; but experience has proved this notion to be erroneous; and Sir Francis Head, a very good authority on these matters, has pointed out, if we mistake not, that the proper place for attaching the girths is in the middle of the saddle. It is, no doubt, quite possible, by placing the girths forward, to accumulate the whole amount of friction on one or two points; but this is precisely what bruises horses' withers without having power to prevent the saddle slipping.

Direct proof of the correctness of what is advanced here may be obtained in the following manner : Take a longish saddle on which the girth-straps (or points) are fixed forward; girth the horse tolerably tightly; now put a rider in the saddle—the heavier he is the more apparent will the result be—and get him to sit *well* back. You will find, by putting your fingers flat between the girth and the horse's chest *before* the man mounts, that, on his taking his seat as above, the girth will be drawn forcibly *upwards;* a proof that the saddle must have relinquished in a corresponding degree its previous "gripe" of the horse's back, or rather shoulder. Now let your man dismount, loosen the girths a little, and put a surcingle right over the *middle* of the saddle ; draw this equally tight as the girth had been previously, and put your rider once more into the saddle, making him, however, sit exactly in the middle over the surcingle : your finger, if placed as before, will now tell you, if it should not be apparent to the eye, that the surcingle has become *looser*, the saddle has assumed a more intimate contact with the horse's back throughout, and is sure not to slip or wound.

The Hungarian Puszta rider, or cattle-herd, and most Orientals, never use anything but a surcingle, the great advantage of which is that, having loosed it to let their horses graze, they can tighten it with one pull, and are in the saddle and well under way whilst one of us is still fumbling at a multiplicity of straps: and moreover, his saddle remains where he put it ; ours seldom does so except by chance. Civilian riders would not approve of the surcingle ; the same end may, however, be attained by putting the girth-straps in the middle of the saddle, and *sitting as nearly as possible over them.* For military purposes girths might be altogether dispensed with and only a surcingle used.

There is an idea prevalent that if the girths are placed as far back as indicated here (over the false ribs), they must interfere with the movement of the horse's chest and lungs much more than if placed well forward over the true ones. This is, however, precisely contrary to fact: the true ribs are firmly supported at *both ends* to make room for the lungs by being drawn forwards: the largest volume of lung lies directly beneath them; the greatest expansion is required *and takes place here.* Under the false ribs lie the thin lobes of the lungs, which increase their volume in a much less degree ; they are therefore supported only at one end, and expand but little, serving chiefly as supports for the diaphragm or midriff. But any one who has not yet arrived at the dignity of a " corporation " may easily convince himself of the truth of this by putting on a tight-fitting waistcoat and playing cricket in it: he will soon find the top buttons gone, and much less frequently the lower ones, whilst a waist-belt will prove a convenience. The point from which the stirrup is suspended has nearly an equal influence on the stability of the saddle, and a much greater one on the form of the seat than the position of the girths. If the stirrups be wrong, all the rest being right will be of little avail.*

* Any defects that may exist in the English cavalry seat, and the

What is the legitimate use of the stirrups besides enabling us to mount our horses? The first and most obvious one is to give the rider *lateral* support, to prevent
his slipping off to the right or left by his seat revolv-
ing round the horse's body as a wheel does round an
axle. In riding bare-backed, or on a saddle without
stirrups, if the rider falls it is most generally to *one side*,
and not directly forwards or backwards; and it is very
evident that the more *directly under the rider's seat*
the stirrups be suspended, the more efficiently will they
perform *this* duty, the resistance offered by them being
perpendicularly upwards, or precisely in the opposite direction to that in which the weight falls, which is perpendicularly downwards; whereas, if the stirrups be
suspended at a distance from the rider's seat, they act
at an angle to the line of fall: they may, and always do,
in such a position change the direction of the fall, but
they cannot meet and prevent it so efficiently as when
placed under the seat. The second use of these contrivances is to enable the rider, for various purposes,
to rise in his saddle by standing in the stirrups. And
here a distinction must be drawn as to whether it is
the rider's object to transmit his own weight indirectly
*through* the stirrups to the saddle at the *same point* at
which he previously applied it directly with his seat,
or at some other point. In the first case it is very
obvious that the stirrups are best placed exactly *under*
the rider's seat; for, putting aside any changes of the
position of his own body from the hips upwards he

very glaring ones that are very obvious in the French seat, and were
the immediate causes of all the sore backs in the campaign of 1859,
depend on the wrong position of the stirrup in the respective military saddles.

may please to make, everything remains as before, and
the equilibrium of the horse is not disturbed.   In the
second case, on the contrary, supposing the stirrups to
be placed far forwards, and the rider far back in the
saddle, standing in the stirrups will at once throw the
weight from one end of the saddle to the other ; make
this press partially on the horse's back instead of equably,
as in the first case, which see-sawing *must* tend to make
the saddle shift, and *must also* alter the equilibrium
of the horse, throwing its weight more forward, consequently rendering the animal incapable of turning
sharply and handily, and, if done suddenly, frequently
even bringing it to a dead halt.   In hunting, sharp
turns are seldom required, whilst speed is ; and therefore there *is* a justification for throwing the weight forwards or backwards, especially in jumping ; but even
this has certain limits, of which more hereafter.   Again,
in road-riding, the English fashion of trotting requires
a man to rise in his stirrups ; but there is really no
reason why he should therefore sacrifice the lateral support spoken of above to the extent one often sees, or
throw such a surplusage of weight on his horse's forehand.   There can be no doubt that he rides *less safely*
by so doing, for a sharp wheel-round of a shying
horse is more likely to bring him down ; but this
question of trotting must be also reserved for a future
chapter.

For military purposes the stirrups *must* be placed in
the centre of the saddle directly under the rider's seat :
there is no alternative.   The cavalry soldier is often
compelled in the use of his weapons to stand in his
stirrups.  If by doing so the equilibrium of his horse be
altered, he disables the animal and himself at the most

critical moment. The power of turning rapidly to administer or avoid a sword-cut or lance-thrust is seriously impaired if the stirrups be placed forward, and the whole concern makes a heavy pitch into the trough of the sea, just at the moment it should "run up into the wind's eye." The late Sir Charles Napier relates in one of his books a lamentable story of a fine gallant English sergeant who lost *both his arms* in this way; and officers who have served in India or Algiers often complain that there is no preventing the native horsemen getting behind their people's backs, where, of course, they have it all their own way, like a bull in a china shop. Sir Charles throws the blame *altogether* on the enormous pack the regulars are compelled to put on their horses' backs. This has, no doubt, its own special influence; but any one who has seen cavalry skirmishing, and understands the mechanism we are labouring to explain, must have also seen that the position of the stirrup acting on the rider's seat has a great deal to do with it.

We mentioned above that the man riding barebacked, or on a saddle without stirrups, most frequently tumbles off to the right or left; well, it will be found that *with* stirrups, especially when the latter are *very far forward and very short*, the catastrophe generally supervenes right ahead, the performer being projected in trajectories, not yet described in ballistic works, away over his steed's neck, to the great damage of collar-bones. It is like having one's hand pierced by

---

* Almost all "rider nations" place their stirrups exactly under their seat. This will be evident from an inspection of some of our Plates, as also that the example has been followed in the best Continental cavalries.

leaning on a reed—the short stirrup that is relied on for safety furnishing an admirable lever-point for the equine catapult.

And this brings us to the length of the stirrup. The length of the arm is generally prescribed as being the proper length for the stirrup. This might answer well enough if stirrups were always suspended at the same perpendicular distance from the upper surface of the saddle, *and* also right under the rider's seat, *and if* men's arms and legs *always* bore a fixed proportion to one another; all of which "ifs" turn out on nearer inspection to be algebraical *x*'s—that is, very variable quantities. To adjust the stirrups *precisely*, the rider had better first mount, and then, letting these instruments loose altogether, shake himself down into the *lowest* part of the saddle, wherever that may be situated; his assistant may then adjust the stirrups to a convenient length. There is no use in attempting to ignore this *lowest point*, because every motion of the horse tends invariably to throw him into it, and if he does persist in ignoring it, he will find himself a mere stirrup-rider, which is, in its way, quite as bad as a rein-rider, the combination of both being the very climax of bad riding—in fact that monkey-like fashion of clinging to your steed vulgarly termed "sticking a horse." For the absolute length of the stirrup no special rule can be given, applicable to all circumstances and to all kinds of riding; in speaking of the different kinds of seats in a subsequent chapter we shall have to return to this point. The only general rule that can be given is, never make your stirrups *so long* as to render your tread on them *insecure*, nor *so short* as to allow them to cramp up your legs and deprive them of the requisite power of motion, making you depend on the stirrups and not on your seat for your position in the saddle. The Orientals all ride in the short stirrups in which they can stand resting on the entire sole of their feet on account of the shovel shape and the size of this contrivance; but their stirrups are hung *directly* under their seat, and in a very different position from that which they occupy in our saddles (see Plate IV). Short stirrups on an English saddle give quite a different form to the seat in consequence.

With respect to the upper surface, or seat, of the saddle, we have to remark, that as the under one must be large in proportion to the weight, so this should be roomy in proportion to the bulk of the rider : a heavy man will always require a large under surface, but not equally constantly a large upper one, for it is bone that weighs ; and as, whatever the seat may be, it should be permanent in some one part of the saddle, there is not only no use, but a positive disadvantage, on account of weight, in having it larger above than is absolutely necessary. It is, however, the form of the upper surface that decides most as to the permanence of the seat. If what we may call the ridge of the saddle be perfectly horizontal, the seat will be determined chiefly by the length and position of the stirrup, because the two surfaces, rider and saddle, are in imperfect contact; and it is therefore usual to dip this ridge at some point and spread it out into a more or less concave surface. Now the form of the seat will depend altogether on the relative position of the *lowest point* of this dip ; if it be placed far back the rider will remain there, and if it be placed in the centre the seat will be also cen-

tral, and for military purposes enough has been said to
show that this is its proper position. Nothing can be
more certain than this, that it is the saddler, and not
the instructor of equitation, that can most effectually
and certainly produce the uniformity of seat which is
so desirable; but unfortunately few people ever think
of this. The sum of the whole matter is this—*the
larger the surfaces of the rider and saddle brought
into permanent contact, the firmer will be the seat, and
the less will it depend on the stirrups or—the reins.*

The saddle-flaps serve in some cases to increase, in
others they absolutely diminish, the surface of contact between the rider and *horse:* their chief use is
to protect the man's legs from injury by the girth-
buckles, straps, &c. For military saddles nothing can
be more preposterous than a stiff flap interposed between the rider's leg and horse's side, because the surcingle and shabrack cover all these things effectually,
and perfectly attain *this* object of the flap of the
English civilian saddle. This stiff flap is therefore an
unnecessary additional weight, and it keeps, moreover,
the leg out of its proper position. To sum up the
whole of the foregoing, we may describe the general
rule for seats to be this,—*the saddle in the centre of
the horse's back; the girths, stirrups, and rider about
the centre of the saddle;* in short,—

> "The maxim for the horsy tribe is
> Horatian, 'Medio tutissimus ibis.'"

There are certain appendages to the saddle that require a short notice. And first of all, which is better,
the blanket or the feltplate under the light cavalry
saddle? The advantages of the former are, that by

folding it in different ways you may vary its thickness at different points, and by this means adjust the saddle not only to all the different peculiarities presented by the backs of various horses, but also equally to the changes of form of one and the same back, induced by changes of condition. You can do nothing of the sort with the feltplate; this presupposes all horses' backs alike, which is very wide of the mark; and, moreover, each individual back permanent in its form, whatever change the condition may have undergone—which is equally so. The blanket men say "Yes; and, more-over, you can defend your horse from the cold in winter bivouacs, and keep him serviceable for a much longer time." * "Ay," say the opponents; "but the man covers himself up and leaves his horse to shiver." There is probably some truth in this; and, at all events, the man is kept warm, whereas the felt can never be misappropriated in this way. The advocates of the felt say further, in cases of alarm the horses can be saddled quicker which is indisputable to a certain extent; for whether the blanket be used as a covering for the horse or man, it takes some time and *two* men to fold it properly if once unfolded. The result is this: if the felt *happens* to fit, the horse will be quickly *and well* saddled—if not, quickly *and badly;* on the other hand, two or three minutes more *may insure* all the horses being *well* saddled, provided the men know how to fold their blankets, and are made to do so. Two or three minutes may be, however, of great importance: let us endeavour to estimate their precise value. Cavalry on

---

* The greatest possible luxury in the matter of blankets is, how-ever, powerless to keep horses alive whose rations consist of their neighbours' tails, as in the Crimea.

outpost duty never unsaddles, therefore it can suffer no loss of time on account of the blanket; and cavalry in camp or bivouac is, or at least should be, always covered by outposts, and is therefore scarcely liable to surprise, and two or three minutes can make no possible difference where it is a question of preserving the efficiency of the horses for weeks, months, and years. But the superior officers are impatient, their personal credit is involved in the turning out rapidly : ay, that's it. Let the blankets be properly folded at daybreak regularly; and let the horses be saddled too with loose girths, whether you know if you are to turn out or not, and there is an end of the blanket difficulty and of many others too.

With regard to the crupper. If your saddle fit properly, and if you sit in the proper way, you don't need a crupper. If neither of these " ifs " be a verity, then the crupper may prevent the saddle running forward, but will also wound the steed's tail, or set it a-kicking, especially if a mare—perhaps, under favourable circumstances, both together ; in either case you must take off the crupper, and what then ? It is better to begin voluntarily with a well-fitting saddle and a good seat, than be kicked into it ; and therefore the cavalry crupper is an absurdity which every one else in the world has thrown away ages ago; and the Austrian, Bavarian, and, we believe, many other German cavalries, discarded some five or six years since.

The breastplate might perhaps, in most cases, be dispensed with ; but in others it is useful in keeping the girths in their place ; besides that, it gives a point of attachment for some of the pack, and is indubitably advantageous for lasso draught; it can do no harm, moreover, unless it be too tight, which is generally the result of cavalry commanding officers being as pedantic about the rosette attached to it being at the same height throughout their front, as infantry ones are about the mess-tins being mathematically correct on the tops of the knapsacks.

# CHAPTER III.

WHEN one observes the great variety of seats on horse-back that present themselves to our notice every day, and their totally contradictory character in the most important respects, a certain amount of bewilderment necessarily ensues, which resolves itself into a curious dilemma. We can scarcely admit that they are all wrong, and it seems equally impossible to assert that they are all right : which, then, is the right, and which the wrong? or is a seat on horseback something outside of the laws that govern the rest of animate and inanimate nature, subject to no rule, defiant of all generalisation, and, in fact, a thing *per se* — a sort of mysterious existence beyond our ken? What, for instance, can be more contradictory than to see one man sitting at one end of the saddle, as in an easy-chair, with his legs tucked up at the other, till his knees are nearly on a level with the pommel ; whilst a second, sitting in his fork, sticks out his legs as stiff and as far away from the horse as he can, taking for his model what is very aptly named in ' Harry Lorre-quer' " the pair-of-tongs-across-a-stone-wall seat"—for an illustration of which see Plate V.? And there are no end of intermediate seats between these two, with the most wonderful curvatures of the rider's back, knowing positions of his head, and artistic contortions of his lower extremities, each and all of which have their partisans and admirers.

We set out with the declaration that we have no desire or intention to set up any one kind of seat as a model; but this is no reason why we should not try to find out and lay before our readers what are the real essentials, leaving them to adopt whatever suits their purpose best. Now the seat on horseback is maintained either by balancing or by friction—that is to say, the greater or less amount of the rider's sitting parts brought into contact with the saddle—or by the support given by the stirrup; and it is easy to perceive that such a combination of *all three* means as leaves *each individual one* its greatest amount of efficiency, will necessarily secure a much greater amount of stability than can be attained by depending on one to the neglect of the other two, or even depending on two in such a manner as to sacrifice the third. The best and safest seat will be always that which depends exclusively on no one means of support, but uses them all in the best manner.

In order to answer the question, Which of the three is the most important? it becomes necessary to review the positive value of each in detail; and first as to balance.

It has been shown, in the preceding chapters, to what an extent the action of the horse depends on the balance or poise of rider and bearer taken together, and how every modification of the latter affects the former, and therefore, that not only some one particular poise must be adopted, but also maintained, for each kind of riding.

E

Again, it has been shown that the stability of the saddle and the safety of the horse's back depend to a great extent on the stability of the rider's weight—that is to say, on his poise or balance. In addition to these two items comes a third one—namely, the value of poise or balance to the rider himself. Why does anything tumble down from the position it has hitherto occupied? because it loses its balance : and the rider that does so is sure to meet the same fate, unless the friction of his seat, the stirrups, or the *horse's mane* are called to the rescue. Can there be any doubt as to the great value of poise or balance? We think not.

As to friction, this depends, in the case of two *inanimate* bodies coming in contact, *first*, on the *nature* of their respective surfaces, which we must leave altogether out of question here ;* and, *secondly*, on the absolute weight with which the upper one presses on the lower one. The amount of surface of contact does *not* increase friction, but, of course, if the whole weight be brought to bear on one or two points of a rider's seat, these will soon require soap - plaster. Here, however, we have to do with an inanimate body, the saddle, on the one hand, and a very lively one, the rider's seat and legs, on the other, whose muscular action may form a very important adjunct to the dead weight in increasing friction ; and the amount of this action *does* increase with the surfaces in contact, because a greater number of muscles are brought into action ; therefore, we can never bring too great an amount of the surfaces

---

* A very smooth surface to the saddle lessens the friction, for which reason school saddles are usually covered with tan-coloured buckskin, whilst many Orientals adopt sheepskins with wool on, coarse rugs or mats, &c.

of our seat and legs into contact with the saddle. The friction arising from absolute weight no rider will be inclined to increase by loading himself. Whether that derived from muscular action shall become an important addition to the former, or merely an independent alternative, is, after all, the great point at issue, and that which constitutes the *real difference* between seats. Muscular action will prove an addition to the friction derived from weight if both be exercised simultaneously nearly at the same point, and in the same direction ; if not, the rider will have to depend alternately on one or the other, instead of both taken together, which is, of course, much less advantageous.

In some forms of seats the rider depends almost entirely on the pressure of his knees against the fore part of the saddle, and relinquishes altogether the advantages derived from steady contact of his seat with the other end of it. For riding a race or a fox-hunt this may answer; but muscular power is subject to waste, and this method will never do for continuous exertion, being much too fatiguing to the rider, and therefore uncertain.

Nor is this all. " Making," as Sir F. Head says, in describing *the hunting seat,** "the knee a pivot, or rather hinge, and the legs beneath them the grasp," is like holding a horse-pistol between the tips of the fore-finger and thumb, instead of grasping it in the full hand. If the weapon kicks on being discharged, it will revolve on the *hinge* with a vengeance ; and if the horse perform a similar feat, the upper two-thirds of the rider's body do the same round the *knee-pivot.* The leg, from the knee downward, is much less

* 'The Horse and his Rider,' p. 31.

fitted for holding or grasping than the thigh is; moreover, it has other functions to perform that interfere with this. The best hunting, steeplechase, and military riders we have ever seen, all agreed in this one point at least—that of depending on the thigh, and not the "under-leg," for their seat; and hence is derived the grand cardinal rule for a good seat : "From the hips upwards *movable*, in order to enable the rider to vary his balance, or use his weapons; from the knee downward *movable*, for the use of the spur, and the control of the horse's hind legs; and between these two points, hip and knee, *fixed*, for the seat." According to this rule, the middle of the rider adheres, both by weight and muscular action, to the middle of the horse; according to the other system, the lower third of the rider clings, by muscular action *alone*, to the horse's shoulders, aided, perhaps, to a certain extent, by the stirrup.

But this brings us to the stirrup. Riding was certainly invented and practised before saddles existed; and it is nearly equally certain that the first saddles, pads, or whatever they were, had no stirrups, these contrivances having been subsequently invented for the purpose of giving the rider further aid in addition to that derived from balance and friction. Even nowadays many a man can ride bare-backed to hounds or in the *mêlée* without stirrups; and this very short statement of facts ought, we think, to go far to prove that stirrups are very subordinate in value to balance and friction *taken together*, which is precisely why we have used the term stirrup-riding in an opprobrious sense. The "tongs-across-a-wall seat" depends on balance and the stirrup, renouncing all contact of the legs with the horse's body; the wash-ball seat goes further, and abjures balance. In Chapter II., when speaking of the position of the stirrup in the saddle, we could only give *some* of the reasons why this should be central. We have now arrived at a point that renders it possible to give the remaining ones, which are of no less importance. They are these: The interior surfaces of a tolerably well-built man's thighs and legs, from the fork to the heels, are curved in concave or hollow sweeps, that may be varied from the *knee downwards* by turning the toes more or less outwards;* and if we look at a horse from the rear, it will be very evident that his midship section—that is to say, the lines we should see if the animal were chopped fairly in two right through his fourteenth vertebra—coincides very accurately with the sweep of the rider's legs. At top, no doubt, the figure is flatter than the man's fork, but the ridge of the saddle fills up the empty space to a certain extent: besides which, no *good* rider sits *in his fork*, but on his seat. Further, although the horse's body is rounded away under the belly, the possibility of varying the curve of the leg from the *knee* downwards enables the rider to preserve contact very low down: he can encircle his horse nearly two-thirds when sitting on this line.

If, on the contrary, the stirrup be placed too far forward, the thigh runs diagonally forwards toward the horse's shoulder. Now let us look at the horse from the front, standing exactly opposite to his forehead. We see at once that the animal's body, besides being narrower

---

* It is therefore very absurd to insist on any specific measure for this. Even a round-thighed man may get up a hollow curve by turning out his toes a little in excess.

at the shoulders than at the midship section, presents, first of all, a concave curve from this to the shoulder, and then a convex one over the shoulder. The former of these has no adaptation whatever to the curve of the rider's thighs, and this he cannot change; to remedy which, the fashion of padding the saddle-flaps was introduced. Sir F. Head says it is going out again. The effect of this padding or increased thickness between the rider's leg and the horse's body is, however, to bring the former, *from the knee downwards*, right away from the latter, as any one can see who looks at this kind of rider from the front; and it is therefore evident that the greatest amount of adhesive surface is obtained by placing the stirrup nearly under the rider, and making the tread on it perpendicular, instead of in an acute angle with the horizon.

There is another point to be considered. Is there anything gained by the rider's leg from the knee downwards being in close contact with the horse's body at the midship section, or lost by its being just behind the shoulder, whether in or out of contact? The gain is simply this, that in the first case we can exercise immediately an absolute control over the horse's hind legs, and make him place them as we please—and these being the propellers, we have entire mastery; whereas the loss occasioned by the stirrup being far forward consists in our generally coming much too late with our leg, when we have occasion to use it in this way, the horse having swerved right round before we can get at him and compel him to go ahead; in our having to pull right against the stirrup-leather; and, worst of all, in our being compelled to loosen our whole seat, in consequence of our thigh-bones refusing to bend. The effect of these two positions of the stirrups and forms of seat on the stability of the latter, when it becomes necessary to stand or rise in the former, we must reserve for a little.

There is a notion prevalent that a military seat is a fork-seat; this is simply a popular error that requires refutation. On the other hand, some people will persist in sitting on that part of their back which is still, perhaps, called back, instead of on that portion of it which is honoured with a supplemental designation. What is a man to sit on? Well, he has two bones in his seat, which we venture, in imitation of German phraseology, to call his "sitting-bones," and a third in rear—that on which umquhile Lord Monboddo built his celebrated theory, since improved on by Darwin, of the human race having been originally developed from monkeys; this third bone completes, with the other two, a triangular basis for the human seat on horseback, and, be it said, a much more efficient one than for the theory in question.* If the angle of the hip-bone comes to be perpendicular over the sitting-bone at the same side, the rider's weight will rest on this triangular basis, which, being the largest available for the purpose, affords the greatest degree of stability to the seat. If, however, the perpendicular from the hip-bone falls *to the rear* of the sitting bone, the leg and thigh are immediately thrown forward to the horse's shoulder, the rider's back is converted into the segment of a circle, and his weight sways about unsteadily on the Monboddo corner of the triangle.

* It has escaped the observation of the Darwinians that monkeys on horseback never sit on their tails, which, of course, upsets their whole theory.

Finally, if the aforesaid perpendicular fall *in front* of the sitting-bone, the fork-seat is achievèd, the thighs come back towards the horse's tail, the rider's body is carried forward by every movement of the animal, because it rests only on two points instead of three, and this may be styled the " muff school of equestrianism."

Whatever difference of opinion may exist as to where the rider should sit in his saddle, or however necessary it may be to vary the exact position of the seat according to the object in view, there can be no doubt whatever that the only firm and steady seat *is on the triangle:* the Monboddo bone must neither be overweighted nor made too conspicuous.

The seat therefore, as such, depends on balance or poise, on the amount of surface brought into contact with the saddle, both of which in their turn depend on whether the rider's weight rests on three, two, or only one corner of a triangle, and all this is necessarily modified by the position of the stirrup. We have endeavoured to show the relative value of each element in succession, and now leave the reader to make such a combination of them as best suits his purpose, reminding him merely that, although he may safely modify first principles, he never can totally despise them without committing an absurdity.

A question presents itself here which, although appertaining more properly to the department of practical instruction, is so intimately connected with the matters we have just now been discussing, that it is impossible to pass it over without a few words—it is this : Should we give our first instruction in riding with or without stirrups ? The advocates of beginning without stirrups say, you must first give the pupil a seat, and then when he has acquired balance and a hold of his horse, you can give him the *additional* assistance of the stirrups. Now the most difficult thing to attain is balance, and the stirrup was devised for the purpose of assisting in acquiring and maintaining it; and it is therefore just as reasonable to act in this manner as it would be to set a boy to learn swimming without corks or bladders, and when he had learned to support himself in the water give him these artificial aids—and this is seldom thought rational. But there is another objection— namely, that the pupil first acquires one seat, and afterwards is expected to change it for *another and better one.* Why not begin at first with this? Every practical cavalry officer knows that it is much easier to teach a man that has never been on horseback than one who has acquired methods of his own, which give the instructor the double work of unteaching and teaching. Of course if the people ride at home nearly in the same way and in the same kind of saddle that they are required to do in the ranks—as, for instance, the Hungarians, Cossacks, and others—this does not apply; but with all western nations of Europe it does. It is highly probable that the English system of hanging the stirrups far forward in the saddle has been adopted, partially at least, for the purpose of adapting these instruments to a seat acquired *without* them—that is to say, to a purpose they were not intended for. Long experience in training recruits has resulted in the conviction that it is much better, and in the end more expeditious, to give the young rider stirrups from the beginning; and when he has acquired a certain amount of confidence and balance you may take away the

stirrups to *perfect* the latter, without running the least
risk of destroying the former.

To return from this digression, and at the same
time bring our investigation of the general conditions
on which a *safe* seat depends to a conclusion, let us
recall to mind the final result of Chapter II. as it
affects the seat. Whatever the form of this may be
in a state of rest, from the moment action ensues the
lever power transmitted through the hind and fore legs
respectively will constantly tend to disturb the rider's
seat *more or less* everywhere, but *least of all* when
this is exactly over the perpendicular line passing
through the centre of motion (the line $E\ F$, fig. 4),
whereas it will be most felt by the rider the more his
seat is placed away from this line, *especially* in rear
of it.

Here are two scraps of newspaper correspondence :
" He never seemed to move in his saddle from the
starting-post till he had won the race ;" and again—
" They still ride as if they formed part and parcel of
their horses : it is the old Centaur-like form."

English gentlemen like to ride with ease, and will
have probably no objection to grace. The former precludes the idea of all *visible* muscular exertion, and
presupposes a feeling of security; the latter is equally
incompatible with slovenliness, affectation, or stiffness;
moreover, steadiness of the hand depends on solidity
of the seat, and this, as we have seen, depends to a great
extent on the not being exposed to *conflicting* movements derived from the horse.

*The Jockey's Saddle and Seat.* — English jockey-
riding is universally acknowledged to be perfection ; it

is, in fact, a specialty in which the English character
is strongly reflected; for although its mere mechanism
may be easily imitated, the cool judgment, energy,
patience, and promptitude that really constitute a good
race-rider, are natural gifts. What interests us more
especially is, that this style of riding is in perfect accordance with the principles we have been advocating:
the saddle is placed just over the fourteenth vertebra,
it is of such small dimensions that the rider can only
sit on one spot,* and under this, or very nearly so, the
girths are attached and the stirrups suspended; nay,
still further, a surcingle passing over the exact centre
of the saddle is generally employed. The length of
the stirrups should, according to the best authorities,
be such as just to enable the jock to clear his saddle
when he stands in them, *but never so long as to make
him depend on the reins in the least for his upright
position;* therefore, when he does stand in the stirrups,
he transfers, through them, his weight to the centre of
the saddle, without, of course, disturbing the general
equilibrium of his horse. When he wishes to bring the
centre of gravity more forward—which favours, as we
have shown, the propelling action of the hind legs—he
does this by bending his own body forward *from the
hips upwards,* and throwing forward his head, his legs
remaining straight down close to his horse; and this
bend is altogether different from that of the rider who
sits far back in his saddle, with his knees drawn up to
the horse's shoulder. When it comes to the finish, the
jock sits down to "ride" his horse, just as a cavalry
soldier *should,* the great difference being that the latter

---

* *Hibernice,* the racing saddle may be described as having only a
middle, and d—l an end at all.

has but *one hand* to ride with.  Much of the success
of starting depends on the rider throwing his weight
forward at the proper moment, and not *overdoing* it, as
good riders well know.  The bridle is a much greater
difficulty with the race-horse than the saddle, but this
we must reserve for the second part of our book.

*The Hunting Seat.*—This is a difficult subject, and
one that cannot be treated dogmatically.  Hunting is
*well* done in a great variety of forms, and then money
is, to most hunting men, a matter of secondary importance.  The great majority only require their horses " *to
go;*" when they are done up they can buy others, and
so on.  Race-riders mount for other people's pleasure,
and large sums of money are at stake : hence the
severe discipline and the carefully-considered *system of
riding.*  The preservation of the horse, too, is a great consideration : the hunting man rides for his own pleasure,
and is only answerable to himself for his expenditure
of horse-flesh.

The author of the ' Handy Horse-Book,' remarking
at p. 99 on the great difference in speed between English and Irish fox-hunting, says "that the sound principles of hunting are repeatedly sacrificed to the un-
natural speed to which hounds are now forced."  There
are, no doubt, many good reasons to account for this.
Most men care more for "the spin" than for the hunting itself, which affords merely a pretext.  Perhaps, too,
English hunting is less a pursuit of the fox than a des-
perate endeavour to distance Thackeray's all-pervading
snob, which seems, however, not always to succeed ; for,
as " Magenta" says, in the paragraph of his book quoted
above, " the hounds are so forced as to overrun the

scent; then, when at fault, the entire ruck of the field have an opportunity of coming up," &c. &c.

But what we have to do with is the seat, and not the hunting itself, which has been alluded to merely because the pace has evidently a good deal to do with the form of the seat. For, in fact, men of fifty years old and thereabout can scarcely fail to remember that the length of our saddles has been increasing constantly with the rapidity of the pace; and although an increase of the bearing surface of the saddle, as has been already shown, is an admirable thing in itself, no great advantage is derived, so far as the horse's back is concerned, unless the rider be placed in the centre of the saddle. But our saddles have been lengthened chiefly for the purpose of enabling us to get *farther away* from the stirrup, so as to use this as a point of support, not against falling to the right or left, but to prevent one's being pulled right over the horse's head in fast galloping and jumping; and thus many riders whose object really is to throw their weight somewhat forward, because this favours speed, actually come to sit almost on the loins of their horses, where they seriously impede the action of the propellers, and are then compelled to throw their body forward in the most inconvenient and unsightly manner.* No doubt if this system were not found to answer the purpose more or less it would scarcely be persevered in. When, however, we find some of the best authorities recommending, and many of the best living riders practising, something very

---

* Sir F. Head says, in 'The Horse and his Rider,' p. 33, " The generality of riders are but too apt to sit on their horses in the bent attitude of the last paroxysm or exertion which helped them into the saddle, called by Sir Bellingham Graham a *wash-ball seat.*"

different, one begins not only to doubt its being even
relatively good, but also to look with a more critical
eye to its positive disadvantages.   They are these : It
involves unnecessary wear and tear of the horse's fore
legs, because the rider's weight is with every bound
thrown forward into his stirrups in the direction $Q\,P$,
fig. 4—that is to say, exactly counter to the direction in
which the arm-bone *ends* its action; whereas, by sitting over the centre of motion, the shock is equally
divided over all four legs, and not on one pair alone.
This is what we meant by saying that a man may sit
far back and still ruin his horse's fore legs.   Secondly, it
is not the safest method, because, if the horse fails with
one or both fore legs, the rider loses *all* his support at
once, the stirrup acting only as a pivot round which,
by means of his stiff leg, his whole body is made, by
the impulse received from the hind legs, to rotate and
perform the catapult experiment.   And if a horse suddenly swerves, turns on his haunches, or comes to a
dead halt at a jump, the rider is most likely, through
the same agency, to continue the original line of movement, whilst the horse adopts a new one, or "reposes."
Thirdly, this method of riding tends very forcibly to
making the horse convert the rider's hand into a
fifth leg for itself, the pull of the head on the rein
coming at an acute angle to the push or tread of the
leg in the stirrup ; and this, when carried to excess,
degenerates into *pure rein and stirrup riding without
any seat*, especially with horses that carry their heads
low.   It is, however, just precisely with a hard-pulling
horse that a curbed bit would be so desirable, and *with
this seat* it is a matter of impossibility to use one.   The
rule for the jockey we have seen is, never, in standing in

his stirrups, to depend for seat to any extent on his reins. Why this should be neglected in hunting is not easy to understand. The Cossacks and Circassians, who all ride with a snaffle, and do wonderful things with it, sit perfectly independent of the rein : any one can make his horse equally light in the hand with a snaffle as theirs are, by making his seat as independent of the reins *and* stirrups, or use a curbed bit in hunting if he pleases. It is the close steady seat that makes the hand light and the horse's mouth soft; and therefore it is much more valuable in teaching to make the young riders dispense *altogether with the reins than with the stirrups*, and may be done sooner.

Apropos of rising in the stirrups,—" either to avoid a kick, or in jumping a large fence, the rider, by merely rising in his stirrups, at once raises or abstracts from the saddle the point his enemy intends to attack, and accordingly the blow aimed at it fails to reach it."* On the contrary, Mr Apperley says, " When hounds find and go away, place yourself *well down* in your saddle, on your fork or twist, and don't be standing up in your stirrups (as formerly was the fashion, *and the cause of many a dislocated neck*), sticking out your rump as if it did not belong to you." Who shall decide when such high authorities differ ? But perhaps the difference is more specious than real. Mr Apperley says, *well down* in your saddle, which we take it will bring a man very near to the middle of that piece of furniture, and probably to the horse's centre of motion. *Here* the necessity for *avoiding the blow* does not arise, it is the point of least motion ; but if a man sits *well back* in his saddle, *à la* wash-ball, he gets much nearer

* Sir F. Head, as above.

to the action of the hind legs, and nothing else remains
for him than a speedy retreat when this becomes dangerous.   Something like this must be the key to this
difference of opinion; for a rifle or other gun that kicks
will only hit your shoulder the harder the looser you
hold it, and perhaps knock you down if you hold it
quite clear, or at least knock the wind out of you.   If
a man sits in the right place he does not need to rise
in his stirrups *for any such purpose;* and if he does not,
the rising in the stirrups, and thereby abandoning his
whole seat, may or may not help him.

Perhaps we should never have attempted writing a
single line about the hunting seat but for one consideration—it is this : The majority of our cavalry, yeo-
manry, and mounted volunteers are hunting men, and
if there really were such an enormous difference between
a *good* cavalry and a *good* hunting seat, as many people
seem to suppose, it would be simply a very hopeless
case.   But is there this great difference ?   Mr Apperley
says, " Be assured that the military seat with very long
stirrups will not do here, however *graceful* it may appear
on a parade."   Fortunately this great authority gives us
in his own book a drawing intended to represent this
graceful seat, which (see Plate V), on closer inspection,
turns out to be Harry Lorrequer's "tongs across a wall."
Well, no doubt, this won't do for hunting, nor indeed,
as far as we can see, for any other good purpose beyond
exhibiting the high polish of a man's boots, spurs, and
stirrup - irons,—the rider being in uniform  scarcely
making his seat a *good* military one ; but of this more
anon. Mr Apperley has, however, given us two other
figures representing his notions of *good* and *bad* hunting seats, which are here presented to the reader.

PLATE III.

BAD AND GOOD SEAT.

On the other hand, there can be no doubt of the total inapplicability of the wash-ball seat to military purposes; and, after all, one comes to the conclusion that the essential difference between any two *good* forms of seat is not so enormous as is commonly represented. If a man " sits on horse ape-like," as the Hungarian phrase is, he will scarcely succeed in any kind of riding; and we believe that the great secret of good horsemanship in general consists in avoiding exaggerations of all kinds. The saddle, the position of the stirrup, and the peculiar object in view, may and must induce modifications of the seat ; but riding is still riding, and the mechanism of the horse's construction cannot be altered by mere fashion.

*Road-Riding.*—The road-rider, although not required to take fences, or permitted to ride at full gallop like the fox-hunter, has his own difficulties to contend with: he has to do his work on a hard inelastic surface, and not on grass fields or ploughed land ; he must be prepared to make sharp turns, and to meet all sorts of provocations to shying and restiveness, of which the hunting man knows little or nothing ; in fact, handiness, safety for himself, and a due regard for his horse's legs, are much more important considerations for him than great speed. It is all very well to say that a roadster or hack should possess the qualities requisite to insure the above, but *all* does not depend upon the horse ; if the seat of the rider be faulty, a break-down will ensue sooner or later.

Let us take the hard road, in the first instance, into consideration. When one body strikes, falls, or impinges on another, to use a scientific phrase, it receives

F

the blow back *sooner* or *later*. This is, as we all know, what is called recoil or rebound; the elastic surface gives back the blow *later* and more gradually; the inelastic one sooner and more suddenly. The horse's leg being elastic, itself receives but a small shock from the elastic turf, this being divided between both nearly equally; on the hard road nearly the whole recoil is transmitted back to the horse's body through its limbs, and this is nearly equal to the weight of both rider and bearer. There are various means by which this recoil may be diminished in intensity, to the great ease of the horse. One of the most obvious is to distribute the weight as nearly as possible over the middle of the horse's back, which is constructed, as we have shown, in such a manner as to admit of a certain amount of elastic action in a vertical direction—in plain words, up and down. Two men can carry a greater weight with an elastic pole on their shoulders than with a stiff one; and if the burden be not exactly in the centre of it, the man to whom it is nearest will get more of the recoil from the ground than the other one. Now, taking into account that the road-rider does not want great speed, and has at the same time an inelastic surface to deal with, there can, we think, be little doubt that, by placing his saddle and himself over the middle of the horse's back, he will save his bearer and himself a large amount of recoil. If, however, in this position he thrusts his *whole* foot into the stirrup, he thereby throws away a further chance; for, by merely resting with the ball of his foot on the bar of the stirrup, his knee being slightly bent, he superadds the elastic action of his own legs at knee and ankle to that of the

horse's, and this is the *legitimate* and useful form of
" *bobbing up and down.*"

A wholly useless and absurd method of performing
this feat is when the stirrup is ever so far away from
the part of the saddle on which the rider sits, for then
there is an end of the elastic action of the rider's leg;
and unfortunately there are some cavalry services in
which this is practised, to the great increase of rup-
tures amongst the men, and broken knees amongst the
horses.

The plan adopted in England is to avoid the recoil
by rising in the stirrups, which of course is the most
sensible way for a man who has to ride long distances
and is not encumbered with weapons. It has, however,
its inconveniences, especially if the stirrup is placed very
far forward; for then, in the first place, the foot being
thrust home in the stirrup, the elasticity of the rider's leg
is not utilised; and even when this is not the case, the
" tread " being oblique cannot have the effect intended;
secondly, the whole seat is abandoned for a certain
time, nothing remaining in contact with the horse
except the leg from the knee downwards, which is of
little use; thirdly, the horse learns to lean on the
hand, for the rider must depend on his reins, for a
moment of time at least, which of course renders
correct bitting impossible; * finally, the rider's weight
is being constantly transferred from the hind to the
fore quarters of the horse. There may be average
equilibrium, but it is never *permanently* in the right
place, and hence the danger; for a sudden start or

---

* Ladies have in general a much lighter hand than men, their seat
is firmer and closer, and their horses are usually properly bitted.

stumble at the moment the rider is in the air, is the most common cause of the accidents that occur so frequently.

Now, in truth, there is no reason why this English system of rising in the stirrups (in trotting) should not be practised equally well, not to say better, with the stirrup near the middle of the saddle instead of at one end. The difference is this, that a much less amount of rise will suffice, and the seat is therefore not only less completely abandoned, but also for a shorter time ; the horse's balance is not destroyed ; and fine bitting may be resorted to.* There is, however, a further peculiarity belonging to this English method that is worth understanding, because the successful trotting of many horses depends on its being so. The " bobber up and down" rises and falls *with each tread* of the horse; the English rider *only with the intermediate ones :* he always comes down on his saddle simultaneously with one and the same hind leg ; and the consequence is, that in trotting after this fashion one diagonal pair of legs is constantly saved from the recoil, and the other as constantly exposed to it in an aggravated form.

Every practical rider must have observed that with certain horses there is a difficulty, in starting to trot, in the accommodation of the rider's rise in the stirrups to the first movements: he will have to feel his way, as it were, to the proper leg, and perhaps be obliged to sit out two or three shakes before he can get at it ; for many horses trot unequally—that is, take a longer stride

---

* The author has done many a mile of hard work in this way in a military saddle with stirrups exactly central ; and ridden to English foxhounds also tolerably well in full military fig in a stiff country.

with one pair of legs than with the other. The rider
should observe this in difficult cases, and try to find
out, which he soon can, with which hind leg he should
rise or fall: men who have this instinct are able to trot
horses that perfectly good riders fail with.

Lieutenant-Colonel von Oeynhausen tells us * that
the veterinary surgeon Träger, of the famous stud at
Trakehnen, has observed that the near hind and off
fore legs of most horses are stronger than the other
two; and he attributes some well-known but hitherto
seemingly inexplicable facts in connection with horses
to this circumstance—as, for instance, that they naturally prefer, in cantering and galloping, to lead with the
near leg, the weight being then supported by the two
strongest limbs (near hind, off fore) ; that spavin occurs
more frequently on the off than the near side; and that
horses in wheeling about through restiveness always do
so to the left, on the near hind leg, &c. Mr Träger
advances in support of his views the well-known fact
that men's right arms and left legs are naturally most
relied on, being also stronger ; and he believes this to
be the case with very many other animals—dogs, for
instance, whose method of going diagonally seems to
prove it. Now it is quite possible that this is also
the cause of what has been alluded to above—namely,
that in trotting after the English fashion the horse
endeavours to accommodate the strong and weak pairs
of legs to the rise and fall of the rider in the saddle ;
and if so, it is worth the attention of practical men.

It is, however, quite clear that if we desire to train

* B. von Oeynhausen, KK. Oberst-lieutenant, &c. ; 'Der Pferde-
liebhaber' (Vienna, 1865), at p. 162—a book that cannot be too
highly recommended.

horses to perfectly equal action on both sides—as is
necessary for military purposes, where all must be
brought as nearly as possible to one standard of action,
or for draught, where the team should trot alike—it will
be better to employ the " bobbing up and down system "
than English riding.   The Americans understand and
apply this in the training of their great trotters : few
English horses can compete with them, because their
trot is uneven.   But of course there is no use in attempting a combination of "wash-ball," or "tongs across
a wall," with " bobbing ;" it will never succeed in
anything but shaking the rider's lungs out : the nearly
perpendicular tread on the stirrup, with an elastic
ankle to break the jolt, is imperative.   The Orientals,
who use shovel stirrups, and stand straight on the entire sole of the foot, never attempt trotting — their
paces are walk or gallop.   Arab horses have, however,
a tremendous trot if you can bring them to it ; but you
must sit like wax, and have the delicate hand of a first-
rate pianist to do the trick ; for nothing stronger than
a single hair from a fair lady's head is fit for a rein.

There exists in many minds a strong prejudice on the
subject of its easing the horse to tuck up the rider's
legs, and that nothing tires it so much as a long dang-
ling weight *under its belly.*   In the first place, it comes
to this, that a giant should not mount a pony ; then,
again, why dangle the legs?   They have a better
chance of lying close to the horse's body if the stirrup
be placed nearly under the seat, which does not involve
their being too long; and further, how if the rider's body
be made to dangle in the air *over the horse's back,* in
consequence of the attempt to tuck up the legs?   This
is still more dangerous : one sees every day horses reel-

PLATE IV.

THE ARAB TYPE.

ing in trot under riders that adopt the very "lofty" English style; the centre of gravity gets a couple of feet farther away from the basis, which is just equivalent to the latter being decreased proportionately. Every one knows that a man with a long back and short legs rides heavier than a long-legged one.

It is scarcely necessary, after what has been already said, to demonstrate over again how conducive to handiness, perfect mastery over the horse, independence of the rein, and therefore good bitting, a central position of the saddle, stirrups, and seat *must* be; and these are, we take it, the conditions under which road-riding may be done *safely* and *agreeably*. High speed *not* being the object, nothing can be gained by throwing the rider's weight forward; on the contrary, it has this further positive disadvantage in addition to those already pointed out. Corns with our horses are as equally prevalent as broken knees, and the latter are very frequently a consequence of the former. Now we have shown (see fig. 2, *C*) that the consequence of throwing the weight forward is to make the horse *overstep* with his hind foot the track of the corresponding fore foot; and this being very much our habit, our horses *do* very frequently overstep, and by so doing the risk is run of tearing off the fore shoes. We have got into the habit of using very short shoes, the web of which does not overlap sufficiently, at the heel, the angle formed by the frog with the wall of the hoof, but falling short, throws the whole pressure *inside* this angle. This is what produces corns. For racing, certainly, and perhaps for hunting, the short shoe may be inevitable, but there is no reason whatever why the roadster should be shod in this fashion, nor even a cavalry horse, except that people *will* persist in either sitting *directly* on the horse's withers, or when they sit on the loins, transferring their weight to the shoulder, through the medium of stirrups hung far forward, every time they rise in the saddle when trotting. Corns and broken knees are totally unknown in the Austrian cavalry, where the shoe is given a solid bearing *on* the angle of the *wall of the hoof at the heel.*

# CHAPTER IV.

Is there such a thing as a standard military seat or not? and is there any real necessity for it, and what? There can be no doubt that a cavalry in some respects technically inferior may achieve, and often has gained, victories over another, not having any fault of the kind. So very much depends on the way in which this arm is handled, and on its moral qualities, that it is quite impossible to say, "This cavalry, because it rides very well, must, or even will most probably, beat that other one, because it does not ride quite so well." Are we then to conclude that the seat and everything connected with it is a matter of minor importance? The old Austrian cavalry regulations contained a paragraph to this effect: "Cavalry that cannot ride (that is to say, well) is a burden to the state;" but we have been often tempted to paraphrase this, and say, "Cavalry that can *only* ride is not less so." Both expressions taken together will then mean, that it is not enough for a cavalry man to be a bold rider; his riding must be done so as to make him an efficient combatant as well: for whatever doubt may exist on account of the almost impossibility of estimating precisely "the other things equal" of the question to be solved, as to whether a cavalry that rides positively well may or may not prove superior *in combat* to one that rides only comparatively so, this much *is quite certain*, that the former will *bring into and retain in the field a much greater proportion of serviceable horses* than the latter, which is in itself an element of success that may be indeed squandered away like all others, but *must*, if properly taken advantage of, confer great superiority. In fact, what we would say to every cavalry officer of whatever nation is this : Your cavalry is very fine : it has done wonders, and beat *all* other cavalries in the world; but it would do still greater miracles, and beat all *the rest* if you only improved your seat, &c., a little more ; besides which it would cost less—a matter of some importance—and perhaps look quite as well as at present.

No one, we suppose, will contend that the jockey style of riding can serve as a model for the cavalry soldier : the kind of work to be done and its duration are totally different. Perhaps the hunting seat deserves more consideration. This much is certain ; it is of great advantage to cavalry to be able to get across a difficult country, and much of its utility will depend on its being able to do this cleverly, and in an orderly manner. This has been recognised and acted on of late years to a much greater extent than formerly, and, as we think, very wisely too. Up to a certain time the *haute école* dominated cavalry riding exclusively, and, no doubt, very reasonably, in the then existing semi-cultivated state of Europe, and under the conditions of combat then prevalent. But both of these have undergone great modifications : and first of all, what the Germans call the " campaign school," was introduced for cavalry purposes ; and more recently still,

PLATE V.

"TONGS ACROSS A WALL."

THE MODERN MILITARY SEAT.

that very indefinite form called the hunting seat, or rather what is supposed to represent it, has been making considerable inroads into the domains of the riding-master.*   All we propose saying for the present is, that the wash-ball seat is evidently not the proper thing for military purposes, whilst, perhaps, "tongs across a wall" may be, in reality, nothing more or less than the progeny of a *liaison* with that respectable old lady the *haute école*—in fact, a mule seat.

Let us pass in review the points of resemblance and of difference between the two kinds of riding.   The former are but few in number, the latter very numerous.   The hunting man rides his own horse for his own pleasure, and does not mind spoiling a steed or two for the sake of maintaining his character as a forward rider.   Cavalry soldiers *must* ride together almost always : what regulates their speed is the average of a whole regiment, and not the swiftness of a single animal.   The Oriental national cavalries won't understand this, and get beaten by riders who, taken singly, are very inferior.   Again, the hunting man's proper work is all done at full gallop ; cavalry does at least five-eighths of its work at a walk (route marching), perhaps two-eighths in trot (manœuvring), and certainly not more than one-eighth at full gallop (in charging).   The conclusions to be drawn are, that even supposing the *so-called* "hunting seat" to be the best for high speed, no Government can afford the waste of horse-flesh it involves, nor

* The father of a young cornet recently gazetted told the author that his son had been advised by a brother officer to conceal the fact of his being a "'cross-country" rider on joining his regiment, as otherwise the riding-master would keep him twice as long under his hands.

would there be the slightest use in doing so. On the
contrary, this style of riding can only lead to loose
and broken charges, *or* to a voluntary abandonment
of full gallop in charging. Further, the fox-hunter
does not require sharp turning, and he has both his
hands at his disposal; whilst the cavalry soldier's life
depends to a great extent on his horse being able to
turn suddenly and rapidly with the aid of one hand.
The *poise or equilibrium of horse and rider taken together can never be too perfect or too permanent in his
case.* One of the great mistakes committed is the supposing that what *is called* a balance - seat is the one
thing necessary. The whole machine must be in
balance, and not the rider alone.

But the greatest difference is in the absolute weight
or load to be carried. A hunting man buys a horse
*up* to his weight; cavalry can do nothing of the sort,
for their horses are compelled to carry any load we
please to inflict on them. People rig out a soldier
with everything that combined bad taste and absurdity
can suggest—put him on a horse that must not cost
over a certain price, and call him a hussar, dragoon, or
lancer, according to the cut of his coat; and so it comes
that what is *called* heavy cavalry sometimes rides
lighter, and is altogether lighter, than what people are
pleased to consider light cavalry.

There must be some average weight determinable
for the average horses and average work of cavalry,
but it is very hard to get at anything like a satisfactory solution of this problem, in consequence of the
great number of unknown quantities involved in it.
Nevertheless, there can be no harm done in attempting,
at least, a statement of the question.

French authorities * tell us that a *good* sumpter-horse, working on a *good* road, can carry 100 to 150 kilogrammes (equal to 15 stone $\frac{1}{2}$ lb., or 23 stone $8\frac{3}{4}$ lb., at a walk, to a distance of 40 kilometres (equal about $24\frac{8}{10}$ English miles) in ten hours. But if the same horse be required to do its work in trot, the burden must be reduced to 80 kilog. (equal $176\frac{1}{2}$ English pounds), in order to enable it to do $22\frac{1}{3}$ to $24\frac{8}{10}$ English miles in a day (of ten hours). If the burden consists of a rider with his saddle, &c., instead of inert matter alone, the horse can do the $24\frac{8}{10}$ miles at a *walk*, on a *good* road, under the greater load of 90 kilog. ($198\frac{1}{2}$ English pounds), and he will only require seven to eight hours. It is therefore evident that it is the *dead* weight of the pack which distresses the horse most; and our own experience of jockeys carrying extra weight confirms this.

Further, a man carrying a weight without the aid of machinery, can transport 44 kilog. (97 lb. 10 oz. English weight) to a distance of $12\frac{4}{10}$ English miles for a day's work; and on comparing this with the day's work of the sumpter-horse, we find that the former is to the latter in the proportion of 1 to 5.

Now it is well understood that a foot-soldier who has to use his weapons cannot carry anything like this 97 lb. 10 oz. English weight, without converting him into a mere "colporteur," the utmost admissible load being 22 kilog. (48 lb. 13 oz.), or *one-third the man's own average weight;* † ánd as the saddle-horse can

* Migout et Bergery, 'Théorie des Affûts et des Voitures d'Artillerie.'

† The Continental cavalries take $145\frac{1}{2}$ lb., or 10 st. $5\frac{1}{2}$ lb., as the average weight. The British soldiers must be much heavier than

carry 90 kilog. 24$\frac{8}{10}$ miles *only* at a walk and on a good road, if we take into consideration that some of the cavalry horse's work must be done in trot and gallop, and much of it on more or less difficult ground, it is probable that 90 kilog. (198½ English pounds) would be quite sufficient load, although the average marches should not exceed 15 English miles per diem, because the irregular food and the exposure to the weather in bivouacs *more* than compensates for the difference of distance.

It seems, however, to be the practice of most cavalry services to put on their horses at least a third—in many cases even more than that proportion—of the animal's own weight. Strange to say, we must go to the manuals of the artillery and pioneers for the weight of the cavalry soldier. An Austrian authority, Baron Smola, calls the average weight of the horse 740 to 864 English pounds; and it has always been laid down as a rule by the best cavalry officers of that service that 200 Austrian or 246 English pounds, = 17 stone 8 lb., is the maximum load admissible. This would be exactly one-third of the weight of the lighter horse, and about two-sevenths that of the heavier one; so that, in fact, if this rule were adhered to, it would make light cavalry heavier (for the horse) than heavy cavalry. But we suspect that both one and the other have transgressed this limit at various times. Very recently, indeed, the Austrian light cavalry has thrown away sabretaches, echabraques, cruppers, pistol-holsters, and no end of other useless lumber, to the great

---

this, probably 11½ to 12 st. The British infantry soldier's kit at present weighs exactly 11.67 kilog., leaving 10.33 kilog., or about 23 lb., for arms and ammunition.

PLATE VI.

THE EXTREME CHAIR SEAT.

THE EXTREME FORK SEAT.

ease of the horses' backs; and the cuirassiers have been all converted into dragoons. Taking 246 lb. as the total weight, and deducting 66 kilog. or $145\frac{1}{2}$ lb. for the average man, there would remain for arms, saddle, kit, &c., 100 lb., which ought to suffice.

The French 'Aide Memoire' gives us $992\frac{1}{4}$ English pounds for the weight of the horse, and $1296\frac{1}{2}$ for the trooper complete; consequently, the burden is $304\frac{1}{4}$ lb., or *less* than one-third: and deducting from this, as before, $145\frac{1}{2}$ lb. for the man, there remains $158\frac{3}{4}$ lb. of *dead* weight. It is no doubt this, and something connected with the seat, which is *very far back*, the stirrups being *very far forward*, that we must look to for an explanation of the sore-back disasters of 1859. It may appear absurd to accuse the French cavalry of riding with a "hunting seat," but in truth theirs *is* an *exaggeration* of a bad one.

A Prussian book * gives 1152 English pounds for the weight of the heavy horse, and 1546 English pounds for the cuirassier completely armed; consequently, the burden is 394 lb., or more than one-third of the animal's weight: and having deducted the $145\frac{1}{2}$ lb. for the average man, there remains $248\frac{1}{2}$ lb. dead weight, or exactly 50 lb. more than Migout and Bergery's estimate of what the total burden should be. The light Prussian horse is set down at 921 English pounds, and the dragoon or hussar complete at 1252 English pounds. Proceeding as before, we find, therefore, that these horses carry 331 lb. $=$ 23 stone 9 lb., also more than one-third their own weight, of which $185\frac{1}{2}$ lb. is dead weight, or within 13 lb. of what the French authority lays down as the total admissible

* Ludwig Schöne, 'Feldbruckenbau.'

burden. Now it is remarkable that, notwithstanding this unfavourable state of things, we have hitherto
heard nothing about Prussian sore-back disasters in the
campaign of 1866, although the cavalry did an immense deal of work ; and this can only be attributed
to a better seat and method of riding than the French,
for the dead weight is absolutely greater.

If anything is to be made of cavalry in future wars,
the burden of the horses *must be* diminished. The most
obvious way is by lessening the dead weight; but why
should not smaller men be selected ? After all, what is
really necessary is, that the soldier *should be tall enough
to mount with ease and to clean his horse.* Anything
beyond that is superfluous.

Let us compare with the above, in order to show
how far a "hunting-seat" method is applicable to
cavalry purposes, some English standards of weight for
flat-racing and steeplechasing, taken at random from
the newspapers. For five-year-olds we find 10 st. 12
lb., or 152 lb., for half a mile flat, and 12 st., or 168
lb., for aged horses. For five-year-olds, 10 st. 12 lb.
= 152 lb., and for six-year-olds, 11 st. 4 lb. = 158 lb.,
for two miles' steeplechase. For five-year-olds, 11 st.
7 lb. = 161 lb., and for an aged mare, 12 st. = 168
lb., for a three-mile hunter's stakes steeplechase. These
are, we believe, fair samples ; but the horses that carry
these weights do it once for all : they are the best of
their kind perhaps in the world, and are trained and
fed in a way quite beyond the reach of cavalry. The
immediate object, too, is to take the most out of the
individual horse for the moment ; in fact, all the conditions are different.

And as to the seat, the hunting rider can adjust his

PLATE VII.

THE OPEN SEAT AND HIGH PACK.

THE CLOSE SEAT AND FLAT PACK.

weight as he pleases ; he may vary his position in the saddle, which constitutes the whole of the dead weight, and need not exceed 14 lb.; his doing so must not necessarily give his horse a sore back or bruised withers. On the other hand, the dead weight carried by the troop-horse is most usually equal to, in many cases greater than, that of the rider ; a shifting of the seat will therefore necessarily destroy not only the poise of the horse, but, what is still worse, that of the saddle —and this is what kills the horses, or at least sends them into hospital. The cavalry soldier's *seat must* be therefore fixed, and not subject to variation; in charging he must bend his body forwards, from the hips upwards, in order to use his weapons, and stand in his stirrups, and this will all suffice to accelerate the speed of his horse. The grand rule is to arrange the saddle itself and the stirrups so that the *rider can only sit in the proper position, that he falls naturally into it, and that it requires no muscular effort to maintain it.* If this be not the case, the moment the man becomes tired, or his horse makes a rapid movement, the whole seat is lost, and the muscular effort that should remain altogether available for the sabre or lance, is expended in endeavouring to maintain or regain an injudicious seat. The true seat is therefore in the middle of the saddle, whose upper surface should be so formed as not to admit of any other one ; then the stirrup must be under the seat, and not 8 to 12 inches in front of it. The English hussar, Plate VII., is evidently expending muscular action *to keep his stirrup in a certain position at an angle to its natural fall, instead of the stirrup supporting his leg as the latter falls.* Such a position is not maintainable for any length of time, or in sharp

G

movement.   In trot, for instance, the soldier, not being
permitted to rise in his saddle, must seek a support
which the stirrups cannot afford otherwise than by assuming an angle at the *other* side of the perpendicular
—that is to say, the tread in the stirrup comes to be in
the direction of the *point* of the horse's shoulder, " tongs
across a wall," and the counter-action is then upwards
in the line of the man's thigh, against which the intes-
tines descend, and produce, if there is the slightest
natural weakness in the individual, rupture.   The stirrups being far forward in the hunting or civilian
saddle is not so injurious in this way, because the rider
evades the shock by rising in the saddle, and this is
just what led to the English way of riding; but the
cavalry soldier cannot do so.

It is all very well to say the man *must* retain the
position prescribed for him; if he is constantly on the
strain to do so, he *simply cannot;* besides which, the
stirrup is actually of very little, if any, use to him.
Two-thirds of the time and the whole of the talk expended in endeavouring to make a man retain an inconvenient seat can be saved, and devoted to the much
more necessary objects of teaching him *how to manage
his horse and use his weapons*, if you make the prescribed seat inevitable, and every deviation from it
uncomfortable; and this can be easily done.

With the light cavalry (or Hungarian) saddle, it will
not do to put a man into it as it comes out of the
saddler's hands, and *order* him to sit in a particular
manner; it is just as necessary, or more so, to make
the saddle fit the man's seat, as to make his coat or
boots fit his body or feet; and this is done, after careful
observation of the seat, by shortening or lengthening

the bearing-strap of the seat, or by altering the lacings, till the seat comes right of itself, when you don't need to correct it in the riding-school. Fig. 5 shows the outlines of those Hungarian saddles. At *a* the bearing-strap of the seat is laced down so as to have its lowest point towards the rear of the saddle, the consequence of which is to throw the rider's seat back on the Mon-

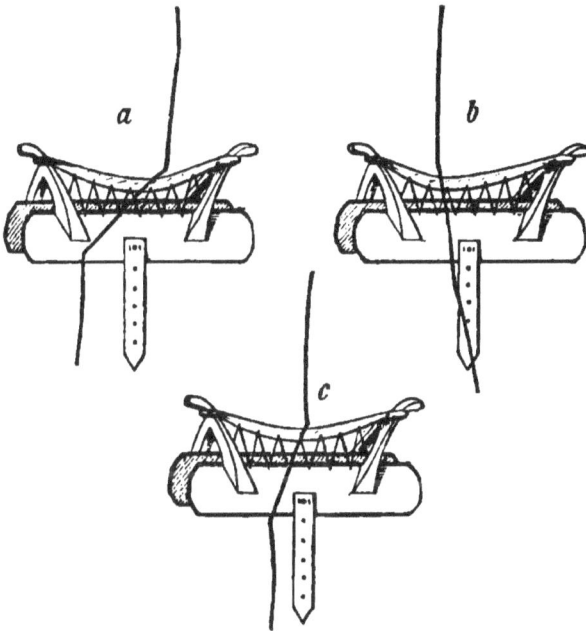

Fig. 5.

boddo bone, bringing the thigh forwards and the knee towards the horse's shoulder, wash-ball fashion. At *b* the reverse is the case; the bearing-strap being laced down in front, its hinder part throws the rider altogether into his fork, and the thigh and leg come too far back, muff fashion: *a* bends his neck and shoulders somewhat forward in order to get his balance, whilst

*b* strains them backwards.   At *c* the lowest part of the
bearing-strap is in the middle of the saddle, all of which
variation depends on the lacing, supposing the length
of the strap itself to be the same : *c* therefore sits on
his triangle with his body upright and his legs coming
down in their natural fall, his whole weight being
spread over the entire under-surface of the saddle-
blades ; whilst it is evident that the weight of *a*, being
far to the rear, will press down the hinder ends of the
saddle-blades into the horse's back, tilting up the front
ends ; *b*, on the contrary, drives the saddle-blade ends
into the horse's withers : *a*'s saddle will probably run
forward, *b*'s horse run through the girths.

The place of the stirrup and its influence on the
seat is here altogether left out of consideration.   It
should be made to accord with the seat, and not the
seat with it, otherwise the rider is always " contending
against " his stirrups instead of " depending on them."

How the bearing-strap of the saddle should be exactly laced will depend altogether on the " plenitude "
or " poverty " of the seat of honour of each individual
rider.   A very full-sized sitting part requires the lacing
to approach that shown at *a* in order to make the rider
sit like *c* ; a very spare man, on the contrary, will require something like *b* for the same purpose ; for most
young men it will do best as at *c*.*

---

* The bearing-strap of the seat is best made of a piece of good
girthing-web, doubled together so as to form, with its central portion, a collar to embrace neatly the hinder knob of the saddle, the
two branches being sewed by their edges together down the middle
of the seat, and ending, the one with a strap, the other with a
buckle, which, when united, form a corresponding collar for the
front knob.   Brass eyelet-holes stamped into the outer edges at
certain intervals would be an improvement.   Of course a movable
pad covers this bearing-strap, the lacings and the side-plate of the

The same principle applies exactly to civilian saddles. If you know yourself how you want to sit, you must tell this to the saddler before he has constructed the seat, as that depends on him and not on the saddletree maker. It is also evident that, if the stirrups of a given tree happen to be hung too far forward, the defect can only be remedied by bringing the lowest point of the seat of the saddle nearer to them, for the tree itself must remain as the rule of thumb turned it out of the workshop. Civilians fancy that a cavalry seat must be stiff and constrained; to be good *it must* be perfectly easy and unconstrained, and then it will not only answer its purpose, but be really graceful.

One of the great difficulties is about the pack. There is no use in putting the saddle in the middle of the horse's back, and the stirrups and rider in the middle of the saddle, unless you at the same time distribute the weight of the pack equably before and behind the latter; the component parts of the dead weight must be accurately balanced against each other. As regards the form, it should be made *as flat as possible*, instead of being built up into two great mountains in front and rear of the rider's seat, and this for the following reasons: First, the nearer the pack is to the perpendicular line falling through the centres of motion and gravity the less will it incommode the horse by its vibrations, tend to displace the saddle, or be liable to break the straps and shake loose itself; and the centre of gravity is most undoubtedly under the rider's seat; therefore, on this account alone, the lower and flatter

saddle, as far down as the tops of the girth at each side, but it is on the length of the bearing-strap, and the way in which it is laced, that the form of the seat will depend. Of course all the edges of these wooden saddles must be nicely bevelled off.

the pack the better.   Secondly, if the pack be high
in rear of the rider, as shown by the English hussar,
Plate VII., the difficulty of getting into and out of the
saddle is greatly enhanced, and with it the chances of
deranging the latter and causing it to turn round;
which leads to overtight girthing.   The Austrian
" hulan," shown on the same Plate, is taken from a
coloured penny picture, the only thing we can for the
moment procure, and is, consequently, *not* so correct as
the hussar, who was photographed from life; still it
serves to show what can be done in making the pack
flat, and adapting it closely to the horse's body.   The
white cloak, it will be observed, is folded flat and
placed *above* the sheepskin, where it can be got at
without opening up the whole pack, and the valise is
also flat.   Why these articles were ever rolled up into
long cylinders, the most intractable and inconvenient
form that can be devised, is utterly unaccountable, except on the supposition of cavalry officers having been
peculiarly subject to softening of the brain, in consequence, no doubt, of the *solidity* of the shakos and
helmets worn in those days.   Thirdly, a mountain of
pack in front of the rider renders it utterly impossible
to adopt a proper system of bitting, or to make the
pull on the reins act in the proper direction; even with
the greatest care and management, the bridle-hand of
the cavalry soldier must be necessarily placed at a
greater distance from the horse's withers than that of
the civilian: we shall, however, have more to say on
this point in the second part of this little work.

The old heavy cavalry leather saddle is gradually
disappearing in almost all services, because it can
neither be adapted to each individual horse nor rider.
There is only one seat possible with it, the chair-seat,

which throws the weight all to one end, and produces sore backs much more frequently than a well-arranged wooden or Hungarian saddle with a proper seat. Several modifications of the Hungarian saddle have been adopted, amongst others, a Danish model; but it is quite absurd to attempt to retain, as has been done in many instances, the chair-seat of the heavy cavalry saddle in a wooden one—better far stick to the old form : however, the difficulty will probably be ended by heavy cavalry being gradually abandoned, for which there are many other reasons than merely the technical ones we have had to deal with.

We cannot wind up this portion of our work better than with a few remarks on the following passage from the 'Handy Horse-Book,' p. 48, 49 : "Altogether it might be desirable that commanding officers of some cavalry regiments would study the pose on horseback of Marochetti's sculptured dragoons, or those of other eminent artists. The result would probably be a marked improvement in the position of the saddle, and, conse-quently, in the general *coup d'œil* of our cavalry," &c. Now, if it were merely for appearance' sake, we should say that no real advantage of other methods should be sacrificed to this; but, after all, what is Marochetti's pose, and why have he and other eminent artists suc-ceeded in producing works that please the eye of such judges of horsemanship as "Magenta" and other sporting men? and why are our public places dis-figured by absurd equestrian statues? Simply because Marochetti perfectly understood the equilibrium of the horse *and* rider, and was bound to do so, as otherwise he could never have got the weight of material to balance on a pair of legs, but must have had recourse, like others, to a post growing out of the ground and into the horse's belly to sustain it, or wholly abstained from the attempt to reproduce his figures in motion. And the ease and dignity of his statuettes depend on the impression they make on the spectator of their perfect security, and because they exhibit the rider as having a perfect control over the movements of his horse; and this is what a cavalry soldier should have. What can be more undignified or repugnant to good taste than to put a great military leader on a horse in the position in which grooms used to ride to water? It disgusts, from being altogether out of character.

But, as we have shown, the safety of the horse's back and the life of the rider—that is to say, the efficiency of the cavalry—depend altogether on perfect equilibrium; and this, we take it, is a much higher consideration than appearance. Fortunately, however, what is really good and to the purpose does please the eye in this as in many other matters. Lastly, far from thinking that a *good* method of riding to hounds is incompatible with, or antagonistic to, a *good* system of military riding, we believe that the former has been of great use to the latter in emancipating it to a certain extent from the pedantry of the *old haute école*, and laying the foundation for the modern system of "campaign riding," which is better adapted to our present cavalry tactics. And, after all, there is not so much difference between a *good* hunting and a *good* military seat as many people suppose; nor should they, on the other hand, be considered identical, as many others believe, the objects to be attained and the means being different. And this is quite certain, that the "wash-ball seat" is just as useless for the one as "tongs across a wall" is for the other. Exaggeration spoils good riding, as it will the best argument, and is ridiculous into the bargain.

# PART II.

# BITS AND BITTING

# CHAPTER I.

THERE is scarcely anything of more frequent occurrence than the transition from an incorrect mode of expression to a popular error ; we see instances of this daily occurring. No doubt the incorrect mode of expression usually arises, in the first instance, either from confusion of ideas or false appreciation of facts, or both taken together ; but when once brought into currency, it is frequently accepted not only as a fitting designation, but actually as a true explanation of the nature or mode of operation of the thing designated, and thus grows into what is called a popular error.

It is more especially in matters connected with mechanical contrivances that we observe this to take place, and the reason is very obvious. Such modes of expression originate with what are called practical men, who, seldom having leisure or scientific education sufficient to enable them to construct at once correct definitions, commonly judge by the eye or the touch, and translate the evidence of one of these senses into a name. It is in this way that the peculiar languages of handicrafts usually grow up, and the apprenticeship to these consists to a great extent in the acquisition of the proper application of such technical terms ; so that, in fact, this sort of language becomes the means of keeping secret certain processes for the benefit of the initiated, and to the exclusion of the general public.

There can be, perhaps, no very serious objection to this in general, the great desideratum being that the workman should know how to do his work properly, not suffering himself to be misled by the kind of mystical jargon applied to it; but there are cases in which it does an infinity of mischief, and tends to the propagation of serious errors. To give a practical illustration: of the thousands that ride and drive horses in this country, but very few have acquired the art otherwise than by self-teaching—what is called practice; and of the nearly equally great number who are intrusted with the care and management of these animals, precisely the same may be said. What shall we say of the somewhat numerous class of individuals that undertake to "break in" horses, as it is called, except that they distinguish themselves generally by an abundance of courage and determination—very necessary qualifications they are, too—and an equally great lack of anything like rational principle to guide them in the exercise of what they have converted into a handicraft. There is a fourth class, not numerous indeed, but very important in their way: those artisans who spend all their lives in the forge or workshop, have seldom if ever any even the slightest knowledge of horses, and still are intrusted with the fabrication of those instruments, too frequently of torture, which we apply to almost the most sensitive part of the animal's body, his mouth.

Now there is scarcely any one expression so common amongst riders, drivers, grooms, and horse-breakers, as that a horse's mouth is hard or soft; and when one comes to inquire into the best mode of attaining the last-named quality, which is, of course, that most desired, we find that the exceedingly sensitive gums of the horse are supposed to become soft in consequence of being subjected to a greater or less amount of pressure from a piece of hard iron ; an idea in itself perfectly monstrous and contrary to fact, inasmuch as long-continued pressure, if not too violent in degree, has the tendency to produce a gradual thickening of the membranes—in fact, renders the mouth callous, or the contrary of soft ; and if so violent in degree as to destroy the textures, and actually involve mechanical softness, the reverse of what is understood by a soft mouth is nearly always produced.

Here, then, most people who have to do with horses start in life with an incorrect mode of expression, which leads directly to a misconception of an important question, and this in its turn to absurd and mischievous methods of practice, and all this from a want of knowledge or a proper application of the simplest mechanical principles. It requires, indeed, only the most superficial inspection of a horse or other animal, either standing or in motion, to perceive that we have to do with a series of much more beautiful and perfect mechanical contrivances than human ingenuity is capable of devising—for the elasticity and power of animal muscle and tendon is altogether beyond our imitation ; and this, applied to a most wonderful combination of levers, constitutes the mechanism of animal power. A little further consideration cannot fail to show us that the means we employ to direct the power of a horse, and make it subservient to our wants and wishes, are altogether mechanical in their nature ; and on entering into an analysis of their mode of action, we find them to consist in the application of the principles of the lever and of equilibrium, matters belonging respectively to the domains of statics and dynamics.

The great difficulty in the rational application of these principles arises partly from the complexity of all problems connected with " equilibrium in motion," and partly on account of the very great diversity in the details of the construction and the relative proportions of these animated machines. If we take the horse's neck, for instance, it may be compared to the tiller of a boat ; it is the lever by which the whole animal is steered, or, in a state of nature, steers itself—the reins being the tiller-ropes. The lever formed by the neck acts on that part of the dorsal vertebræ we have shown to be the centre of motion ; and when the horse is in motion, the lever action of the limbs, derived from the muscles, is propagated to this same point, *the neck and the tail being the regulators* of the movement ; for by means of the neck, the animal, as has been shown in Part I., adjusts its equilibrium according to the degree of velocity it requires, and according to whether it wishes to move on straight or on curved lines ; and a little attention to the movements of young horses, when perfectly uncontrolled, will suffice to show that the position of the neck is constantly varied to suit the exigencies of the moment, the tail following its movements in the most graceful manner as a counterpoise.*

* It would be easy to show that breeds of horses employed constantly for one particular movement have their tails differently seated and developed from those that are employed for a variety of purposes. Our English race-horse is an instance.

It is precisely for this reason that a proper command over the horse's neck is of such value to the rider, enabling him to vary the condition of equilibrium as suits his views for the moment, and to weight one or both of the hind legs, alternately or simultaneously, as may best serve his purpose. It is on a perfect knowledge of this principle that the success of handling young horses, or the overcoming the vices of those that have been injudiciously handled, depends; and there is no more frequent cause of restiveness or indocility than an abuse of the lever action of the neck with young animals.

Some years ago a great sensation was produced by a system of riding, or rather handling horses, introduced by M. Baucher, a French riding-master. According to this gentleman, the power of resisting the will of the rider, and therefore the seat of all restiveness, is located in that part of the neck which forms the articulation with the head; and he found that, by getting the horse's head into a particular position, and fixing it there, he could more or less perfectly master the volition of the animal. But it soon appeared that M. Baucher's system had the radical defect of destroying all the horse's paces; and the Duc de Nemour's condemnation of it, or rather the sentence he passed on it, " Je ne veux pas d'un système qui prend sur *l'impulsion* des chevaux," was most perfectly justified.*

Now the error into which M. Baucher fell was this: The horse's neck is, no doubt, a very powerful agent in our hands; it is, as we have already shown, the lever, and the only one too, by which we obtain a command

* This, too, was the error of the Duke of Newcastle's system, which drove us into the opposite extreme.

over the entire motive mechanism of the horse, especially the hind legs; but it is *only by varying its
position that this can be usefully effected*—by suiting
this to the pace, and the direction of the animal's
movements; whilst M. Baucher insisted on *one invariable position of the head and neck*. Moreover, the
pull on the reins was *not* in the direction of the centre
of motion, and could not act with precision on the
hind legs; finally, the position of the horse's head
and neck were such as rather to increase than diminish
the overhanging weight of these members. Compare
fig. 3, Part I., with the French hussar *à la* Baucher
in Plate VI., which also shows the immense height and
bulk of the pack, and the seat of the rider altogether
on the hinder part of the saddle, although no doubt in
exaggeration. Baucher's "handling" was almost all
done when the horse was standing still, and its effect
either became null when the animal was put in motion,
or, if preserved, the power of locomotion was seriously
impeded. No horse ever voluntarily assumed such a
position of his head and neck as that prescribed by M.
Baucher—in fact, it was wholly unsuited to any form
of movement; it was like attempting to steer a ship that
had no way on her. He overlooked altogether the problem of equilibrium in motion, and *mistook diminution
or restriction of motive power for a perfect command
over it, under all circumstances and at every degree of
speed*. It is unnecessary to add that the demon of
restiveness, whose habitation he fancied he had discovered in the neck-joint, and whom he constantly
attempted to exorcise, was simply the creature of his
own phantasy.

The various purposes to which horses are applied,

demand, of course, different details of handling; but one broad principle applies to them all—namely, to get the whole lever power of the animal to-act in conjunction with its weight in the required direction, and this with such a degree of leaning on the bit that the power of controlling all its motions with certainty and ease is secured, without the necessity of interfering in so abrupt a manner with the animal's efforts as to impede them unnecessarily; and to do this in such a manner that the peculiarities of the individual horse and of his work are brought gradually into harmony, is the only effectual means we possess for avoiding all occasion for restiveness, and constitutes rational handling, as distinguished from purely empirical horse-breaking as it is usually practised. For this is the true secret, and not such violent methods as those employed by Mr Rarey and others. Do not, if possible, give your horse an opportunity of resisting your will successfully, which is usually a consequence of your demanding from him something either beyond his comprehension or capacity; and should restiveness once occur, go back immediately to something the horse will do, and, if necessary, commence the whole process *de novo*.

It will be well to explain here why the perfectly fresh and sensitive mouth of the young horse conveys the sensation of hardness to the hand of the rider, and why the same mouth, after it has really been rendered more or less callous by the application of cold iron to its delicate organisation, comes to be called soft.

When a horse is mounted for the first time, the equilibrium of the whole machine is disturbed, which becomes especially remarkable in the neck. The young horse bores on his bridle, and tries to acquire a new point to lean on—a fifth leg, in fact: he is hardmouthed. But when the animal has learned how to carry *itself and the rider*, or acquired an artificial equilibrium suited to the altered circumstances, then it no longer seeks this support, and the mouth is called soft. That such is really the case can be very satisfactorily proved. A horse can be brought into perfect equilibrium under the rider without any bridle whatever, merely by using a cavesson instead; and if a snaffle be then put into its mouth, this will be found to be exceedingly sensitive, and it will require some days' riding before it will "*take the bit*," as the phrase is.

From what has been just stated, it will be easy to understand how the seat of the rider comes to exercise so great an influence on the horse's mouth that the same horse will go light with one and heavy with another rider. First of all, it is a question of equilibrium. One rider assumes a seat that favours, another one that more or less seriously impedes, the efforts of the horse to get into balance—for horses always try to do this. But, secondly, supposing the seat, so far as the distribution of weight is concerned, to be identical, the unsteady rider will seek a support for himself in the reins, and the horse immediately bores against this, and becomes a hard puller; whilst the steady seat makes a light hand and a soft mouth.

It is, in like manner, easy to understand why not only individuals, but whole breeds of horses, should be found naturally light or heavy in the hand, which is owing mainly to the general framework being more or less favourable to equilibrium in motion—mainly, but not wholly, because the interior conformation of the mouth has always a certain influence, and this is scarcely identical in any two horses, even as merely regards those points that have a direct bearing on the working of the bit; and, moreover, because temper and even sex have also to do with it.*

It is abundantly evident, from the foregoing remarks, that the question of bits and bitting cannot be solved without reference to the whole theory of riding and draught; in fact, it forms a very important part of both, which must serve as an apology for the contents of this introductory chapter. Indeed we must go a step further in this direction, and call the reader's attention to another item. What has been said on the subject of the lever action of the neck will suffice to indicate that the direction in which the pull of the reins is made to act on the centre of motion, through the medium of the head, must necessarily determine both the direction and intensity of the lever action transmitted in succession to the other parts of the animal's frame. It is in consequence of this that by merely elevating or depressing the hands, employing a certain amount of pressure with the rider's legs, and throwing his weight backwards or forwards, that it becomes possible to make the horse alter the conditions of his own equilibrium, by bringing his hind legs more under him, or the contrary. In like manner it is possible, supposing the pull to be horizontal—which is,

* It will be necessary to go into further detail on this point in a subsequent chapter. In the meanwhile, we cannot refrain from observing how absurd it is to attempt rigid uniformity in the patterns of bits used by cavalry, or, as is not unfrequently done, continuing through a long series of years the use of a bit originally destined for a very different kind of horse from that found in the ranks at the present day.

by the way, the normal direction for a well-set-up horse for cavalry purposes, as we shall presently see— to concentrate the lever action on *one* of the hind legs in preference to the other, by simply throwing our weight slightly to the same side, which enables us to fix, as it were, certain legs to the ground, or detain them longer in contact with it, setting the others free, and determining with accuracy the mode and the moment of their employment. Many horse-breakers do all this by a sort of instinct. In fact, if they could not do it they would scarcely ever succeed in handling a horse; but there are very few uneducated riders who comprehend precisely the rationale of these processes, and are capable of effecting them in all cases with certainty, which is, however, indispensable to success in the handling of young horses, or retrieving the mistakes that have been committed by others with older ones.

We may say, then, that the art of bitting and bridling is a very useful and essential one, because it enables us to avoid the infliction of pain, whilst it secures to us a perfect control over the horse's movements. It consists in enabling us to exercise the mechanical action of the reins in the proper degree and the right direction, for every horse and for every movement.

The influence of good and judicious bitting and bridling on the breaking-in and training of horses is incalculable, whilst ignorance on these points, and abuse of these instruments, are a very frequent cause of restiveness, and of the ruin of young animals, especially of highly-bred ones with their delicate organisations. A bolting race-horse may be set down pretty nearly with certainty as one that has been mismanaged and abused in this respect. It is scarcely credible the amount of terror with which some horses regard the bit, and the blind fury with which they take it between their teeth, throw up their heads, and bolt in consequence.

Considering the great number of "unthinking" riders and drivers that exist in all parts of the world, it seems perfectly miraculous, when one looks at the frightful instruments of torture placed, in the absurdest manner, in their horses' mouths, and used in the most wonderful ways, that so few accidents occur. It is only a proof of the admirable tempers of our horses. The Irish ones are frequently deficient in this respect, being still more grossly abused. But still one sees every day, in broken-kneed horses, lamentable evidence of the perversity and ignorance with which horses are treated in this great horse country. There is no use in mincing the matter: this is, to a great extent, a consequence of ignorance of the true principles of bitting, saddling, and—riding; for a broken-kneed horse is an opprobrium to its rider.

As regards cavalry, few things are so important as good and careful bitting. The steadiness of a troop or squadron in its evolutions, and especially in skirmishing, charging, and rallying, depends mainly on it. The writer of this has on more than one occasion converted, in the course of a few days and at a very moderate expense, a body of this kind that had become almost unserviceable from bad bitting into a model of steadiness, the bolters and restive horses all disappearing as if by magic. No doubt, in order to effect this, every single horse's mouth must be measured, and fitted in the manner to be explained hereafter. Three or four sizes or patterns will not suffice for even 160 or 180 horses, much less for a whole regiment, although our Cavalry Regulations lay it down as a rule that each *regiment* should have "a *few* bits with different and easy mouthpieces and curbs, &c."

Draught-horses are, on the whole, less absurdly bitted than those used for the saddle in this country; and the huge bits one sees sometimes in the mouths of those devoted to purposes of show and pleasure, although ridiculous enough from being so wholly out of proportion, have their reins usually buckled into the cheeks, so as to render the lever action of these wonderful specimens of ironmongery perfectly nugatory, which is so far fortunate. It is, moreover, strange that it should be the fashion to "bear up" carriage-horses to a state of balance which more nearly approaches the equilibrium of the manege than anything else, whereas draught requires the centre of gravity to be carried forward, and the weight thrown somewhat more on the fore legs. And having touched on this point we may as well say a word or two on the subject of the blinds attached to the bridles of harness-horses. All of a sudden a movement seems to have sprung up in favour of abolishing this appendage, which is asserted to be both cruel and useless. Now, in fact, it is neither the one nor the other, but, quite on the contrary, it has a very decided use, and from rendering the management of horses easier, it tends to save them from the infliction of punishment. The horse's hind-quarters are the portion of his frame most open to attack, and the animal's instinct renders it consequently extremely jealous of every approach in this direction, which it is prone to resent rashly by lashing out with its heels, with or without real provocation. It would be, no doubt, a great cruelty to deprive a horse, by means of blinds, of the faculty of providing for his own safety when this care was naturally thrown upon him. But this is not the case with a draught-horse in harness; the driver is there to assume this charge: and the certain consequences of taking blinds off will be to make a great number of horses kickers, and to cause numerous accidents to occur from horses running away to avoid some white apron or handkerchief or the like that appears in their rear. Teams of artillery-horses without blinds become in consequence unapproachable in column by officers who have to gallop up and down with orders; many a leg has been broken in this way, and many artilleries have introduced blinds in consequence, and with immediate effect. Horses without blinds are always for starting off before the driver has a hold of the reins, and soon learn to kick at the least motion of the whip.

But enough has now been said to prove the great importance of well understanding the principles on which bits and bridles should be applied and constructed, both as a means of insuring to the rider and driver perfect command over their horses, and also of saving these most useful and docile animals from ill treatment and unnecessary pain.

# CHAPTER II.

WE have spoken of the horse's neck as being a lever, which of course, strictly speaking, supposes it to form nearly a straight line, and to possess only a very limited amount of flexibility, neither of which properties, in fact, perfectly belong to it.*   But a well-shaped neck, well clothed with firm muscles, possesses both straightness and inflexibility sufficient to render it possible to apply to it the theory of lever action with perfect propriety.   Such a neck will only deviate from the straight line to any considerable amount near its point of junction with the head, this latter also acting as a lever, and imparting to the whole that graceful curvature so pleasing to the eye even of the uninitiated—which is, however, not merely a matter of taste, being, in fact, an evidence of perfection of equilibrium and power.

It is scarcely necessary to say that there are almost infinite varieties of necks to be found amongst horses as regards these two very important items of straight-

---

* The horse's neck really forms a double curve, one being turned upward, the other downward ; the mechanical action results in a straight line forming the axis of the whole.

ness and inflexibility; it will, however, suffice for our present purpose to point out two extreme cases, the one of form—the ewe-neck; the other of want of stability—the long, straight, thin neck, scantily clothed with flabby muscles. The annexed figure shows how the direction of the pull of the reins is modified in each instance, and how this in its turn changes the

Fig. 6.

direction in which the neck acts on the back. We see that with the exaggerated ewe-neck the lever action goes downwards under the withers immediately on to the fore legs; with the long thin neck that bends throughout like a fishing-rod (as also with all horses broken and bitted on Baucher's principle), it goes upwards through the withers into the air, in both of these cases missing altogether the centre of motion;

whilst the intermediate position, combined with the requisite degree of stability, affords a pull in the desired direction, and, coupled with the weight of the rider, meets directly the action of the hind legs, the source of all propelling power.

Nor is this mere theory, for every one that has mounted a great variety of horses, and paid even a moderate degree of attention to their different styles of action, will at once recognise here the true reason of the star-gazer appearing to have his fore legs nailed to the ground by the lightest pull on the rein, whilst the croup and the hind legs are flung wildly about, no pressure of the rider's leg being capable of steadying them and keeping the brute straight, either at rest or in motion. Again, who that ever rode one of those long thin-necked, unstable, rainbow quadrupeds that are so apt to dazzle the eye of the uninitiated, can ever forget the slipperiness of all its movements, and the painful sensation of being mounted on a machine composed of gutta percha and glass? all of which, making due allowance for the irritable tempers of such horses, is a necessary consequence of the pull of the reins being in a wrong direction.

Let us look at cavalry horses. The soldier has one hand for the reins and the other for his weapon : his efficiency depends altogether on his being able to use the latter with precision and rapidity; and this is an impossibility, unless, to use Sir Charles Napier's words, " the steed watches the edge of the weapon "—that is to say, follows the lightest movement of hand and heel instantaneously, as it were intuitively. The Minister of War of a certain German State once represented to his sovereign that it would be necessary to give the whole of the cavalry sabres of a new pattern, the existing ones being *two inches shorter* than any others in use in foreign services, which would put our troops to great disadvantage : quoth his Excellency, "Then let my cavalry soldiers get two inches nearer to their opponents than has been hitherto the practice," replied Serenissimus. It is just this, it is an affair of inches; and these inches are widened into yards when the horse does not or cannot follow the reins instantaneously and accurately.

We have already pointed out several disadvantages of the mountain of pack that is built up on the shoulders of some cavalry horses; an additional one is, that it changes the line of direction in which the pull of the rein acts, so as to make it go right up into the sky, and altogether miss both hind and fore legs, thus placing all horses, whatever the excellences or defects of their organisation may be, on the same dead level of uncertainty and inaccuracy. It is not the weight alone of " the epitome of a Jew's old-clothes shop " that is so destructive, although this in itself is bad and absurd enough ; what is still worse is the way in which that weight is distributed, so as not only to render all attempts at equilibrium impossible, but also to throw the bridle-hand of the rider so high that he cannot use any description of bit advantageously. A Cossack will load his horse to almost the same pernicious extent that most regular light cavalry men are compelled to do, and still neither the speed, the agility, nor the power of endurance of the little animal are impaired in anything like the same degree as happens with the troop-horse : the weight is better distributed for all purposes.—(Plate VI.)

No doubt it is scarcely possible to avoid some degree of pack on the front part of the military saddle, but it is precisely for this reason that it is so highly important to give the head of the troop-horse a proper position, which can only be maintained by very careful and accurate bitting, after that of the neck has been attained by a judicious system of riding and breaking-in; and still one is astonished to see the pack of the officer built up into the same absurd form as that of the private, although there is no necessity whatever for this being done.

The reader perceives, by these frequent and unavoidable digressions, how intimately the question of bits and bitting is interwoven with the whole system of breaking-in and riding horses, especially for military purposes; and he will see farther on the great importance of this point, particularly when we come to discuss the immediate action of the bit on the interior of the horse's mouth.

We have next to consider the animal's head in connection with this question. Hitherto we have, for the sake of greater convenience, always mentioned the neck as the lever by which the rider controls the motion of the whole animal; but a simple inspection shows that the head is the lever by means of which we gain a command over the neck, and its size, weight, the manner in which it is set on to the latter, and other particulars, have each of them its own share of importance. It is scarcely necessary to say that a very large heavy head renders it a matter of extreme difficulty to get the horse into anything like equilibrium, and big-headed horses will be therefore generally, although not always, heavy in the hand; but it by no means follows from this that small heads confer of themselves the opposite quality; in truth, more depends on the way in which the head is set on to the neck, the make and proportions of the latter, and the facility thereby afforded for assuming a great variety of positions, than on the absolute size of the head itself.

Generally speaking, all our British breeds have well-formed and well-proportioned heads. Irish horses, however, have frequently large ones, and what is of still greater importance, peculiarities of conformation which, in consequence of ignorance and injudicious management, sometimes tend directly to produce restiveness, or other equally unpleasant results.

It will be well at this point to call attention to a very simple mechanical principle connected with lever action—namely, that the effect produced depends not only on the absolute power applied, but also on the direction in which this is done. For instance, considering the horse's head as a lever which is to act on the neck and bring it towards the rider's hand, it is very evident that if the former be so stretched out as to form, as it were, a continuation of the latter, as we see race-horses coming into the post, there is, in fact, no lever action whatever. In the same manner, if we can imagine the horse's chin to be brought under, so as to touch his neck, there would be very little, if any, lever action. This is greatest when the head is at a right angle with the neck; and the more it departs from this line,—either forwards, when the animal pokes out its nose—or to the rear, when, in consequence of severe bitting, or other causes to which we shall presently advert, it touches its breast with its chin,—the less will be the useful lever action on the neck.

In fact, we always see runaway horses assume either the one or the other of these two relative positions of the head and neck, the lever action of the head on the neck, and of the latter on the centre of motion, being in both cases reduced to a nullity, which deprives the

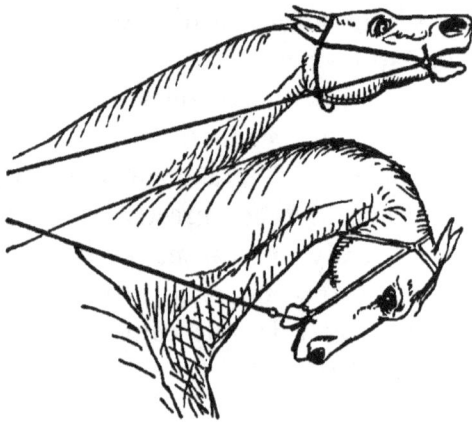

Fig. 7.

rider of all command over his horse; for it cannot be too often repeated that we can only master the horse and obtain a perfect command over his movements by getting the point on which his hind legs, the organs by which he propels himself, act completely under our control, which shows the absurdity of universal bits and all such contrivances.

With the great majority of horses, the physical conformation of the jaws opposes no obstacle to the head assuming the most desirable position; but there are some, and sometimes very good ones in other respects, where this does occur. Let us take, in the first place, *the depth* of the jaw-bone, measured perpendicularly to the forehead on a line passing through the eye: this dimension is sometimes so great in proportion, that if coupled with a coarse, fleshy, short neck, the angle of the jaw coming in contact with the latter, a jam ensues before the head can be brought round to the proper angle. But this is perhaps a less frequent, and certainly a less serious, occurrence than another to which we must now advert.

A horse may have a moderate-sized or even a small head, and the depth of jaw alluded to above may be so trifling as not to offer the slightest impediment to the former assuming any position that may be desired, but the jaws may both converge *inwards*, instead of diverging slightly, as they should ; consequently the space contained between the two jaws is narrowed in, which prevents the neck fitting into this cavity to the same extent as it will in a perfectly well shaped head. The angle of flection in such narrow-jawed horses is very limited indeed, and becomes a serious impediment to the breaking-in and bitting of the animal.

There is another case still worse than this, and not unfrequently combined with it—in fact, the narrowness of the jaws very frequently becomes its exciting cause. Most persons conversant with horses must be aware that certain glands lie just under the angles of the two jaws, and run up in the direction of the ear. They are the seat of the affection peculiar to young animals known under the name of strangles. Now it is by no means unfrequent, especially amongst the commoner kind of horses, to find these glands large and flabby in their textures. With well-bred and well-formed animals it is often very difficult to find them at all under the skin. Sometimes the abnormal size of these glands is evidently constitutional, sometimes it is a consequence of disease—strangles, for instance —and sometimes it arises wholly from the pressure of the angles of the jaws, especially when these lie too close together, and the rider or driver has attempted to force a certain position, either by the use of severe bits, or, what is still worse, a combination of these with the bearing-rein in harness.

If such a state of things be overlooked or neglected, very serious consequences may arise. The forced pressure of the jaw-bone on these glands is sometimes perfectly excruciating to the animal, and it has recourse, to the great astonishment of its ignorant rider or driver, to all sorts of expedients to get rid of the intolerable pain. It will refuse its work, or run away, or throw itself down, or rear up, or do anything or everything in its desperation, and the brute on its back or on the coach-box knows no other remedy for it than " to flog the sulk out of him," whereas the whole thing is probably the result of bad bitting and bridling.*

Many young horses, too, have been prematurely blinded by undue pressure on the glands in question, between which and the eye there is an intimate connection, both by the absorbent vessels and the nerves. We sometimes find the glands affected on both sides, and just as frequently only on one. The horse will in this case exhibit what may be termed one-sided restiveness, bending and cantering perfectly willingly on the one hand, and refusing more or less obstinately on the other. We can perfectly recollect the case of a

---

* Why should not corporal punishment be inflicted on those who disgrace themselves and our common humanity by ill-treating animals ? It would be the nearest possible approach to retributive justice, and much more effectual than fine or imprisonment.

THE NECK, THE HEAD, ETC.

remount where both horse and rider, excellent tempered, willing creatures, had been tortured for months,
until casually passing by we saw from a distance of
fifty yards, by the shape of the horse's head, which
was very prominent, what the matter really was ; on
inspection there was found a regular necklace of swollen and highly sensitive glands, especially on the one
side.

All these peculiarities of formation *must* be therefore taken into account when we set about bitting or
breaking-in horses, and many of those who take this
little book into their hands will be able to call to mind
instances that came within their own observation tending to confirm most entirely what is here stated, and
some will no doubt have cause to regret that they did
not study this subject more accurately before they set
about horse-breaking.

We now pass on to the other parts of the exterior
of the horse's head that have to do with the matter
in hand.   On referring to Plate I., exhibiting the
internal framework and the external contours of the
horse, the reader will perceive, on looking to the head,
that the osseous or bony parts of this organ are covered
very unequally by the soft parts—the muscles, skin,
membranes, bulbous roots of the hair and beard, fat,
&c.—in fact, what are usually called the integuments ;
the bone has, moreover, sharp edges on the under surface of the lower jaw, and a certain portion of the
nose consists of cartilage, as may be seen from the
Plate already referred to.   The practical importance of
all this depends on the different degrees of sensibility
to pressure that result from these varieties of conformation ; for instance, the lower lip is covered with a

very thick skin, underneath which lie the roots of the beard, fat, and membrane, and this structure is continued up into a certain depression under the chin, known as the chin-groove, and called by the Germans the curb-groove (*kinnkettengrube*). Now the portion of bone immediately beneath the thick and not very sensitive skin of the chin-groove is flat and rounded off in all directions, being, in fact, that point where the two branches of the jaw begin to unite together; and if a flat curb-chain, for instance, which has a proper width, act in this groove, a considerable amount of pressure may be applied without causing any very unpleasant sensation to the horse.

But if we pass our finger up out of this groove towards the angle of the jaw, we immediately find that both the character of the bone and that of the skin covering it have become very much changed; the former has got sharp hard edges, and the latter, being no longer furnished with beard, will be found to be thin, and very sensitive; so that a very slight pressure of this thin skin on the sharp edges of bone causes very considerable pain. We shall presently see that no horse can be properly bitted unless these peculiarities be borne in mind and due allowance made for them.

As to the cartilage of the nose, it is of importance to recollect what we are pulling at when we put a cavesson on a young horse; the point at which the bone ceases and the cartilage commences is especially sensitive and liable to injury. A cavesson is a most admirable instrument for those who know how to use it; but most frequently it is like putting a sharp razor in the hands of a madman to let an ignorant or half-taught rider catch hold of the lounge. Many a young

horse has been spavined by an angry drag at his nose
with this very powerful instrument—a good illustration,
by the way, of the lever action of the horse's neck on
his hind legs.

The interior of the horse's mouth is the object that
next demands our attention, but there is only a certain
portion of it with which we have here to do.  It is
easy to perceive, on looking at a horse's mouth in and
outside, that the lower jaw consists of two flat irregu
larly triangular cheek-bones, whose anterior branches
form a groove or channel in which the animal's tongue
lies, enclosed towards its root between the two rows of
molar or grinder teeth, further forward by those portions of the jaw that lie between the point where the
molar teeth cease and the incisors or cutting teeth
commence, known generally as *the bars*, and on the
lower portion of which the tusks are to be found in
male animals ; the channel being closed in front by the
incisors, and the tongue thus fenced from injury on all
sides.

The bit, of whatever kind it may be, coming to be
laid *somewhere* on the bars, and across the tongue, these
are the most important parts of the mouth to be acquainted with.  With the snaffle the portion of the
bar exposed to pressure varies according to the pull on
the reins ; with a regular bit furnished with a curb,
this should not be the case ; in fact, rational bitting
demands that the action of the bit should be confined
exclusively to a certain point on each side, and it will
be shown further on that the bit cannot act properly
on any other point than this one.

We have a rule of thumb in this country for determining the place of the bit—namely, at a certain

height above the tusk ; but as mares and even many
geldings have no tusks, this is a very clumsy method,
which is supplemented in practice by hanging the bit
in the horse's mouth nearly as high as the angles of
the lips will allow it to go.    This is about equally wise
as it would be to put the lock of a gun somewhere near
the vent—an inch or two higher or lower does not matter.    As far as the bit itself is concerned, half an inch,
or even a full inch, higher or lower, would not make
much difference in its action ; but, as we shall presently
see, the curb has one fixed position in the chin-groove,
and this governs the whole arrangement.

There are three dimensions of the interior of the
horse's mouth which must be accurately ascertained
before attempting to fit him with a proper bit, in addition to certain details connected with the tongue.    The
first, and a very important one, is *the transversal width
of the mouth* from side to side, measured *at the same
height as the chin-groove,* and including the thickness
of the lips—that is to say, from the point *d*, fig. 11,
to the corresponding point at the off side.*    This gives
the width of the mouthpiece, which must be made to
fit exactly, as, if too narrow, the lips are subject to
injury and their being displaced so as to cover the
bars, thereby neutralising the action of the whole
instrument ; whereas, if too wide, it slips from side to
side and displaces what is termed the port—the curved
portion of the mouthpiece intended to moderate the
pressure on the tongue—from its proper position : it
also determines the length of the curb.    The second
dimension is the *width of the channel* in which the

* The proper mode of ascertaining all these dimensions accurately
will be stated further on.

tongue lies, or the distance between the two bars inter-
nally, which determines how much of the mouthpiece
may be allowed for the port ; the remainder must be
reserved for the action on the bars.

The third dimension is what we term *the height of
the bars*,—that is to say, the distance between a straight
edge supposed to rest on the upper surface of the bars
at *d*, fig. 11, as above, and another straight edge placed
exactly parallel to it, and touching the undermost
point of the chin-groove—mathematically speaking,
the tangent to the curve formed by the groove.   This
latter dimension—the height of the bars—is perhaps
the most important of all, because all the remaining
dimensions of the bit must be deduced from it.

The width of the mouth is, as may be supposed, a
very variable quantity, depending on the breed and
size of the horse.   Nevertheless Lieutenant-Colonel
von Oeynhausen,* who has had occasion to measure
the mouths of a very great number and variety of
horses, says,† that with the great majority of horses of
the smaller medium size, 15.1 to 15.3 hands high, their
dimension amounts to 4 inches.   With very small and
very light horses one finds occasionally $3\frac{3}{4}$ inches ; the
great majority of good-sized saddle-horses, 15.3 to 16.2
hands, have $4\frac{1}{4}$ inches, and some very large ones go to
$4\frac{1}{2}$ inches ; while 5 inches is only to be found amongst
very heavy draught animals : and on reducing these to
English measure we have 4.148, 3.889, 4.407, 4.767,
and 5.185 English inches.

* Of the Austrian army—perhaps the most learned man living
in the matter of horse-flesh, and the author of several admirable
works.

† ' Zäumungs Lehre,' p. 19.

Our own experience, which has been considerable, though not to be mentioned in comparison with Von Oeynhausen's, confirms this very accurately; and on referring to old pocket-books devoted to notices of this kind, we find that, out of some 400 horses belonging to certain squadrons of light cavalry, measured some eight or nine years ago, the width of the mouth was for the smaller ones exactly 4 English inches, and for nearly the whole of the remainder 4.2 inches, one or two only reaching 4.3 inches. A great number of bits were put down for alteration as being a half to one inch too wide, and some thirty or forty went to the heap of old iron, as being utterly useless from their immense size. Some officers will perhaps smile at this as a piece of pedantry; but if they had witnessed the results obtained, they would probably adopt the same plan. As it is, let any cavalry captain in the British service take the trouble of ascertaining, which he may easily do, how many bits in his troop are half an inch, a full inch, or perhaps still more, too wide, he' will probably then find a clue to many little annoyances he meets with during drill.

The width of the channel in which the tongue lies always bears a certain proportion to the height of the bar, measured as above described ; we must therefore take this latter in the first instance.

Lieutenant-Colonel von Oeynhausen says that the height of the bars is $1\frac{3}{4}$ inches* with the very great majority of horses, and that it is very unusual to find it either more or less. The author has certainly never found bars that exceeded 1.8 English inches in height, but he has seen some that were less—perhaps about

* Equal exactly to 1.81 English inches.

two to three per cent of the horses he has had to do with. Now this is a very important dimension, because the upper bar of the bit should *never exceed* the height of the bar of the horse's mouth—why, shall be made clear in another chapter; notwithstanding which, it is only necessary to go into any saddler's or bit-maker's shop to satisfy one's self that a very large proportion of bits, even of those intended for saddle-horses, are constructed in total defiance of this rule, and calculated for animals that have much higher bars, wherever they are to be found.

But if there is very great uniformity in the absolute height of the bars, there is, on the other hand, a very great diversity in their shape and texture, some being flat-topped and broad—others, again, presenting a ridge-like surface ; some also spongy, soft, and comparatively devoid of feeling, whilst others appear firmer, finer, and more sensitive ; all this exercising an immense influence on the bitting.

The width of the channel for the tongue, or lingual canal, as the anatomists would say, is pretty nearly always three-fourths of the height of the bars; and this being very constantly 1.8 inches, the other will be found to be about 1¼ inches of our English measurement, which gives us the dimension of the maximum *width* of the port of a bit, where there is one; because, supposing the mouthpiece to have exactly the proper width, if the port be made wider than the lingual canal, its corners will come on to the bars of the horse's mouth and produce intolerable pain, which, once for all, is wholly inconsistent with good bitting : and this is precisely the reason why it is of so great importance that the width of the bit should coincide so accurately with that of the horse's mouth; as, if it be too wide, and a port exists, every pull of the rein will be sure to bring its angles into painful contact with the bars on the one side or the other.

The tongue itself is what we have next to direct our attention to. This organ will be found to vary very much both in thickness and texture. In some horses it just fills its own canal neatly, rising towards its axis in a gentle curve, whose summit is two-tenths or three-tenths of an inch above the level of the bars; in others it seems much too thick and fleshy for the interior of the mouth, and projects in all directions. Now the volume of the tongue is a matter of very great importance, because the action of the mouthpiece is divided between this organ and the bars of the mouth; and the great nicety in bitting is practically to determine for each individual horse how much of the lever action is to fall on the tongue, and how much on the bars.

We started with the proposition that lightness or heaviness in the rider's hand depends *mainly* on the degree of equilibrium that the horse may have attained; but the reader will perceive that what is called softness or hardness of mouth must depend, to a certain extent, on the dimensions of the bit corresponding accurately with the interior conformation of this organ. The most perfectly adapted bit will not convert a raw remount at once into a trained horse, or give him a proper carriage and feeling—all this is done gradually with the snaffle; but when the horse has once acquired the carriage and the degree of feeling that may be required, *then* no pains should be spared in bitting him correctly, otherwise all the previous labour is lost.

And this brings us to a very difficult and very important point. Each style of riding, to use a common expression—or every particular kind of service that may be demanded of a horse, to use a more correct one—demands a corresponding variety of carriage and degree of feeling, and consequently of bitting. On the three older continents we find the following styles predominant : School-riding, as a preparation for the circus or for military purposes, and what may be called natural riding. What we understand by this latter is not how the farmer jogs to market with a sack of wheat behind his saddle, but the methods of riding adopted and transferred from generation to generation amongst those nations or large communities who are compelled to live on horseback, either in self-defence, or to gain their existence, or for both reasons. This is, in fact, uncultivated military equitation ; and the purely empirical principles on which it is founded are such that they readily accommodate themselves to the scientific principles of school-riding, with which it, however, only comes in contact in the east of Europe, if we except, perhaps, our own Indian possessions and Algeria.

Cossacks, Circassians, Hungarians, Poles—these are the European and western Asian representatives of the style of riding alluded to here. They furnish its best and most easily formed light cavalries, heavy cavalry having been originally the parent, and subsequently the pupil, of the school or manege. But in the west of Europe this nursery for light cavalry has long ceased to exist. Perhaps the latest remnants of it were the Border-riders on the Scotch and English marches. Indeed, the few civilian riders that were to be found in France,

Germany, Italy, Belgium, Holland, &c., till within comparatively few years, were riding-masters' pupils of one kind or another; and it was only in the British Islands that a numerous class of natural riders was to be found. The Continental riders have had, therefore, all more or less of a military or school type. There existed until recently only one general style of riding, saddling, bitting, carriage, and feeling amongst them, varying, however, very much as to correctness in different countries. Of late years, no doubt, a great change has taken place in this respect, and what is called *English riding* has been more or less successfully imitated *or* caricatured in various parts of the Continent.

Now the English type of riding has been formed by the national sports of racing and hunting, both of which require vehement straightforward riding in the first instance, and only a certain amount of handiness or dexterity in turning; and it is, therefore, neither desirable, nor indeed practicable, to give either the neck or head of the horse anything like the same position that other styles of riding admit of or require. *Therefore the system of bitting must be different to a certain extent.*

In fact, whenever it is possible, the jockey prefers riding his horse with a snaffle, and the best hunting-riders seem to be of the same opinion; and when they do use a curbed bit, it is most generally either as a sort of reserve for particular emergencies, or in combination with a bridoon (using all four reins), by means of which the action of the bit is very much weakened. There are, however, a great number of racers and hunters whose tempers, or desire "to go," require the perma-

nent use of a curbed bit, and hitting off the proper form
and size of this is sometimes a matter of great nicety;
for the bit that will prevent bolting, and enable the
jock to ride a waiting race, may interfere with the
horse's starting freely, or "laying himself out when
called upon." No doubt the jockey that has a very
close and steady seat, and places himself on the right
part of his horse's back, will be able to ride almost
every horse with a snaffle, because, being independent of the reins for his seat, his hand is light,—and
this is the secret of snaffle riding. Still, it is often
a matter of convenience or necessity to use a curbed
bit, and it is therefore important even for the race-
rider to know exactly on what principle its action
depends.

Again, with the hunting man, the bit that enables
him to hold a runaway may interfere with the horse in
jumping. If he be not a mere rein and stirrup rider,
he can no doubt get on best with a snaffle ; but many
a man does not like the labour of holding a pulling
horse, and therefore prefers a bit. The difficulty a good
rider that prefers the bit will have to contend with is
to avoid the getting *too powerful a bit*, or the putting
a suitable one into a part of the horse's mouth where
it must act contrary to his intention. Well, what we
profess to show is, that *light bits accurately fitted* are
more to be relied upon than the most atrocious instruments of torture ever invented, and of which but too
many are in daily use.

But we must, in justice to ourselves, say here, once
for all, that we know of nothing that can be done in
the way of bitting for the man that depends for his
seat on his reins—or on his stirrups, which comes to

the same thing. The rider with a really good steady seat can jump his horse with precisely the same bitting that suits the school-rider or cavalry soldier, if he simply take a very long hold of the curb-rein with his bridle (left) hand, and use the right hand in front of it so long as his horse requires being "kept straight," and then the moment the horse rises to the leap, takes the latter away, leaving the horse to jump *altogether without* any feeling on the reins, which will *insure* his landing on all four feet instead of two only ; but this requires a seat.* And it is precisely for this reason that it is absurd to talk of cavalry and hunting riding being antagonistic. The latter, if *well* done, confers boldness and vehemence in charging, and a disregard for common obstacles; but it should not be overdone or caricatured, for that would lead to bad skirmishing and slow rallying after the charge, by means of which great efforts of gallantry are frequently neutralised and converted into disasters, of which it would be easy enough to cite instances.

For the road-rider good and careful bitting must always have an especial value, restiveness being but too often the consequence of the contrary ; handiness and perfect control being an essential to safety, and great speed not being required, therefore the roadster not only may but must be better "set up" and more finely mouthed than the hunter. Here, too, the grand thing is a seat independent of reins and stirrups, without which the best bitting will be of little value.

---

* This system has been practised in Hanover for the cavalry with great success, according to General von Dachenhausen, but we ourselves used it many years since, and without being aware of this fact.

What should the *carriage* of the cavalry horse be?
for this is what determines the bitting. It must
favour the short sharp turnings and *voltes* of the
school, without impeding the straightforward rush of
the hunter; therefore the adjustment of the weight
*and* the bitting must be such as to enable the horse
to pass from the one style to the other, when required,
with ease to itself and the rider. The rule of the
manege is, that the frontal line of the head (forehead and nose) should be perpendicular to the horizon, the neck being brought up so that the mouth,
and consequently the pull on the reins, should be on
a line with the horse's back, so as to allow of the latter
acting directly on the centre of motion. There are,
however, but few horses so perfectly formed in every
respect as to be able to assume this carriage and *maintain it in all their paces.* We have already pointed
out the obstacles likely to arise from the conformation
of the neck, head, and throat, and we may say that
not one troop-horse in a thousand is capable of being
brought to this standard of carriage, if it were necessary, which is by no means the case. We must therefore take a lower one, or rather one more universally
applicable, and perfectly sufficient for the object in view.
No better rule can perhaps be laid down than that of
Lieutenant-Colonel von Oeynhausen, who says:* "I
consider, as a general rule, that position of the head
to be best with which the horse's paces are *clean* and
*free*" (to be clean they must be equable and their
rhythm perfect; to be free they must be made without
apparent effort or marks of distress); "which allows
him to turn willingly and without an effort or dis-

* 'Zäumungs Lehre,' p. 10.

turbance of his pace; to diminish or increase this without hesitation; to rein back, preserving a proper degree of feeling, and immediately to advance again freely if called upon."

Now, although a star-gazer with a ewe-neck, or a borer that can only go with his nose close to the ground, are totally unfit for military purposes, we must take average horses, and allow one to poke out his nose a little more than another; nor can we always help its coiling up its head and neck like a snail, so long as they go *clean and free*—which is precisely what Baucher's *encapuchonné* carriage of the head and neck does not favour; but the higher we get both head and neck without sacrificing *cleanness and freedom* of pace the better, if for no other reason than that there always must be *something* in front of the military saddle which keeps the bridle-hand at a certain distance above the horse's withers, close down to which the civilian rider can easily place it. Carriage is, however, not the result of bitting alone, it depends, as we have already shown in Part I., on a judicious system of saddling, packing, and riding, the bitting forming "*le couronnement de l'édifice*," without which the remainder is of comparatively little use to the soldier, because he must *ride altogether with one hand*, and he requires his whole body, from the hips upwards, with the exception of this one hand, for the use of his weapons.

Good bitting, saddling, packing, and riding, are what render cavalry available and durable; they secure efficiency, and therefore economy; of course they cannot insure judicious handling of the arm, nor affect the *morale* of the soldier beyond giving him a sense of security and power, which is, however, very valuable.

· The reader will perceive, from the digression into which we have been led here, that the question of bitting cannot be considered separately from those of distribution of weight, carriage, and action; and it was in order to avoid erroneous impressions on this very point that we have thought it best to defer up to this moment all mention of those peculiarities of the interior construction of the horse's mouth which, taken together, constitute, so far as this organ itself is concerned, what is called a hard or a soft mouth.

There are two ways of expressing what a soft mouth is; we may either say this horse goes well on a light bit—which may be mainly a consequence of good carriage, temper, &c.—or we may say, a light bit will probably suit this horse best, *because it has a thin tongue, high and sharp bars, a wide tongue-channel, and fine lips.* But, in truth, the relative thickness or thinness of the tongue is the main point to be considered, because, as has been already pointed out, the height of the bars is very nearly the same in all horses, and the width of the tongue-channel always bears a certain proportion to it. No doubt the bars have in some instances a flat and in others a sharp or convex upper surface, which, together with the greater or less fleshiness of the lips, makes a great difference; but in the end it comes to this, Does the tongue fill up its channel merely to the brim, projecting only a few lines over the surface of the bars, and therefore permitting the mouthpiece to exert a certain degree of pressure on the latter? And this we would call a naturally soft mouth, so far as interior conformation goes.

A hard mouth, on the contrary, will be one in which

we find a thick fleshy tongue, not only totally filling
up its channel, but protruding over it, and rising high
above the level of the bars, which makes the former
appear narrow and the latter low, whatever their real
dimensions may be; and if to this be superadded a flat
surface to the bars and thick fleshy lips, we may forth-
with set this down as a case in which an ordinary
mouthpiece will exert its pressure mainly on the tongue
and lips, conveying to the rider's hand the dull feeling
of pulling against lead.

As a general rule, well-bred horses have the first-
named conformation of mouth, and common brutes
the contrary one; but it by no means follows from
this that the former are all light and the latter all
heavy in the hand : for the most aristocratic animal
of all, the English race-horse, has generally a good
tough mouth of its own, because it is taught from
earliest infancy to lean on the bridle, and seek a fifth
foot in the rider's hand; whereas, on the contrary,
we often find a perfectly plebeian brute, with a tongue
that overfills its mouth, and everything else in proportion, not only extremely sensitive to the action of
the bit, but in fact totally averse to its contact —
that is to say, "behind the hand," because it has
miserable flabby muscles, unstrung tendons, and weak
hind quarters.*

All this tends to show that it requires a considerable
deal of judgment, practical knowledge of horses, and
perfect understanding of what is required in each

* A dishonest horse-dealer that really possesses talent will always
avoid showing you a horse with an incipient spavin or other defect
of the hind legs otherwise than on the lightest possible bridle:
three-fourths of these arising from "savage bitting."

especial case, to enable one to undertake the task of selecting and fitting bits with any chance of success; whereas it is a matter that is most usually intrusted to certain classes of individuals who possess no other qualification than the habit of wearing green baize aprons or nether garments of a very peculiar description—viz., saddlers and grooms.

# CHAPTER III.

THE cavesson, not being a bit, is mentioned here only because some riders are in the habit of commencing the handling of young horses with this instrument, which, although most useful and admirable in the hands of a really skilful person, is equally dangerous and destructive in those of ignorant and brutal horse-breakers. If a young horse be lounged, it may be well to continue the use of the cavesson for a day or two after the operation has ceased, putting in hand-reins for that purpose, so that the animal may be gradually accustomed to the snaffle ; but it is a great mistake to continue its use for any length of time in this way, because the horse learns thereby to lean into the rider's hand, which is what should be avoided from the very commencement. When used for the above purpose, the cavesson should have its nosepiece buckled just low enough to rest on the point of the nose just above where the cartilage joins the bone, but particular care must be taken to prevent the cheek-straps injuring the eyes, which they are very liable to do.

Of all instruments employed in the handling, riding, or driving of horses, the common smooth snaffle is by far

the best and most generally useful; it is that by means of
which the highest results can be obtained, whilst, on
the other hand, less mischief can be done with it than
with any other.    There are some few riders whose seat
is so firm and hand so delicate that they can venture
on putting a curb-bit at once into a horse's mouth, but
these are rare exceptions ; and although, in former
times, it was the custom to bit and curb the cavalry
remount at once and send it to its work, especially in
war time, this system, which produced almost as many
restive horses as all other causes put together, has
been finally abandoned everywhere, except amongst
the Orientals, and the greater part of the handling is
now done on the snaffle.

The great value of the snaffle is, that by its use the
horse acquires confidence and insight into the means
by which the rider proposes to direct its motions, and
that it willingly assumes a steady and regular feeling,
the action of the mouthpiece being gentle and capable
of gradation ; and, in consequence of its acting on nearly
the same part of the mouth as the curb-bit, it becomes
a much better preparative for the latter than the cavesson can ever be, whilst it can never act in so violent a
manner as either the one or the other.

It is precisely for this reason that the simplest form
of snaffle—neither too long, too thin, nor too much
curved, and with only one joint in the middle—is the
best ; but as there is no end of fancy and prejudice
about various kinds of snaffles, it will be perhaps well
to see into the real effect of some of those varieties of
form and dimension that are so much relied on by the
knowing ones.    If the snaffle mouthpiece were simply
two straight pieces of iron of equal thickness through-

out, jointed together in the middle, its whole pressure
would, with most horses, come to act on the tongue
exclusively, and, the base of the mouth remaining un-
touched, there would be therefore scarcely any action.
To avoid this inconvenience, it is usual to make each
half of the mouthpiece thicker towards the cheeks,
and tapering off finer to the joint connecting them, by
which means a portion of the pressure is transferred
from the tongue to the bars; and, in addition to this,
they may be slightly curved, which has the same effect.
Let us suppose the length of such a snaffle to be just
sufficient to allow the cheek-rings to come clear of the
lips on either side, and we shall have nearly the whole
action of the instrument exerted in the same direction as
the pull on the reins,—a matter of no small importance,
because it is the only true basis for an understanding
between the horse's mouth and the rider's hand.

We may make our snaffle very thin in the centre,
and very thick on each side, but we scarcely gain anything in power by so doing, because, although a greater
amount of action is transferred from the tongue to the
bars, the thick portion of the iron acting on the latter
produces very little impression; this variety of form
might, however, prove useful with a slight-built horse
having a very thick tongue.

Another plan is, to leave the thickness of the iron
unaltered, but increase the curvature; or to increase
the length of the whole snaffle, so that it projects an
inch or more at each side.  Now either of these plans
will, no doubt, increase the painful action on the bars;
the latter especially, much practised by Irish horse-
breakers, if exaggerated, will convert the snaffle into
an instrument of torture; but the result of this in-

creased action is in a wrong direction—it ceases to be a fore-and-aft pull, and is converted into a pincer-like twitch on the lower jaw, which becomes so painful that the horse tries to get the mouthpiece on his teeth, which is usually resented by sawing, restiveness being the most common result.

Some riders have recourse to a double-jointed snaffle, others again to a double mouthpiece, the joints being placed right and left of the centre ; but these two forms produce the pincer-like twitch, and are therefore to be avoided if possible.

There is one abomination that cannot be sufficiently reprobated—namely, a snaffle twisted on one side and plain on the other, the pretence for using it being, that the horse is hard-mouthed on one side.  Now it has been already pointed out that this disinclination to turn to one side is sometimes produced by a swollen gland under the jaw, or by a narrowness of the jaws themselves ; and when anything of this kind is the cause, it is evidently pure brutality to apply sheer force. But many horses dislike turning—to the right, for in-stance—where no local impediment of this kind exists; and here it will be found, that circling in trot on the right hand, first of all very wide, and gradually nar-rowing in, the rider's right hand directing the pull of its rein towards the horse's *left hind leg*, whilst his left hand keeps the horse's head and neck *up* to the proper position, is a much more certain and also humane mode of attaining the end for which ignorant riders employ the one-sided twisted snaffle.

A snaffle twisted on both sides is a much less objec-tionable instrument, and may be safely used by *a well-tempered* and judicious rider who has a firm seat ; it should, however, be scarcely ever necessary to resort to this or any of the above-mentioned methods of increasing the painful action of what should be as nearly as possible a painless instrument,* because there are other and better means of attaining the same object.

Better means, because they are more durable in their effects, although they may require more time in the first instance; for, apart from all other considerations, there is this great objection to all the contrivances referred to here, that when you take them out of the horse's mouth you find yourself at best just where you were before, and still more likely not nearly so well off, because the animal's temper will have suffered.

In the great majority of cases, when a man finds that his horse lies heavy in his hand with a plain smooth snaffle—in fact, when he cannot hold him—he looks out immediately for something sharper—a twisted mouthpiece, or some contrivance of the kind—and seldom takes the trouble to examine how it is that the animal contrives to set the cold iron at defiance. If he did so, he would generally find that this is accomplished by getting it out of its proper place on the bars, and shifting it up to the thick part of the tongue, which the horse can do only when there is nothing to prevent his opening his mouth as wide as he pleases; for, if he can do *this*, he *can* always set the rider at defiance. In former times a noseband used to be employed, even with snaffles, for the purpose of preventing this; but the noseband has been very generally abandoned, ex-

---

* It cannot be too often repeated, that the first object to be attained in handling horses is to gain their confidence, and to lead them by degrees to an understanding of the rider's wishes, which they will always readily fulfil, if they are able.

cept on military bridles or harness, at least in this country.

The chief reason given for abolishing the noseband was, that it was supposed to interfere with the horse's breathing, especially during the long-continued gallops of the hunting-field, &c.; and it was on the same account considered to be, *a fortiori*, wholly unfit for racing purposes. This was, perhaps, not a good reason for rejecting it altogether during the first handling of young horses, as it would have been easy to lay it aside afterwards when they came to their field work; but the truth is, that the noseband was placed so high up above the angles of the horse's mouth that it could not prevent the animal opening its mouth and doing what it pleased with the bit, unless it was buckled so tight as really to interfere seriously with the respiration, even at the more moderate pace of a trot or walk—besides other imperfections, to which allusion shall be made lower down. This was long a stumbling-block in the way of the rational treatment of colts and fillies, and was probably what led indirectly to the invention of various instruments of torture known by the name of " capital mouthpieces ;" but this difficulty has been at length got over, and we are in possession of a contrivance which enables us to effect what the old-fashioned noseband never could.

This is the training-halter (Reithalfter), invented, we believe, by Lieutenant-colonel von Oeynhausen, of the Austrian cavalry, or at least introduced by him into the Central School of Equitation at Vienna several years since. To understand perfectly the great value of this halter, it is necessary to allude to one more disadvantage of the old-fashioned noseband, in addition to those already enumerated, which was, that when the reins of the snaffle came to be shortened, the cheek-pieces of the headstall bulged out to the right and left up to the point at which they were held fast by the noseband, and being stopped there, a certain proportion of the pull on the reins was transferred from the mouth-piece to the noseband, where it, of course, was wholly inoperative; so that this latter, instead of promoting the action of the former, actually interfered with it, making the horse lean still more on the hand than hitherto.

It is as well to mention here that the method now introduced of passing snaffles, used for draught-horses, through rings at the lower end of the cheekpieces, instead of buckling them on directly as heretofore, is grounded on the same principle—that of making the action of the mouthpiece altogether independent of the noseband.

But these ring-snaffles do not, of course, prevent the horse opening its mouth too wide, nor can the old-fashioned noseband do this effectually either; the train-ing-halter does so most efficiently and in the simplest manner. It consists of two cheek-straps whose upper ends are made fast in the buckles of the snaffle-head-stall.* These cheek-straps support, by means of two rings, a noseband composed of three pieces: 1. The noseband proper; 2. A strap about 7 inches long, sewed into the ring on the off side; and, 3. A shorter strap, 2 to 3 inches long, and terminated by a buckle, which is sewed into the ring on the near side. The cheek-straps are buckled into the headstall outside, so

* It is, of course, necessary for this purpose that there should be a buckle on each side.

that the noseband comes to hang below the rings of
the snaffle, and the two back straps are then buckled
together, so that the longer one comes to lie in the
chin-groove, as a curb would with a bit, leaving, of
course, a sufficient play to the horse's under jaw, without allowing the animal to open it beyond a certain
distance, and thus securing perfect independence to the
mouthpiece, and permitting of its acting in the proper
place and direction.

It must, however, be well understood that this halter
is not intended to be permanently employed ; its great
value is, that it enables us, by preventing the young
horse from escaping the action of a light snaffle mouthpiece, to avoid the necessity for employing sharp ones :
in fact, all violent measures are thereby rendered unnecessary during the period of training or handling ;
and when this is once over, we may lay aside our
halter, and either use the plain snaffle, or put a curbed
bit into the animal's mouth, which has been by this
very means perfectly prepared for either ; and that this
is a real advantage we must admit.*

It is scarcely necessary to remark that the snaffle
should neither be pulled up *too* high in the horse's
mouth, nor suffered to hang down *so* low as to interfere
with the tusks or front teeth ; its proper place will be
about one-fourth of an inch below the *angle* of the
mouth ; and in this position a plain smooth mouthpiece, if aided in its action by the training-halter, will
be found to answer every purpose, and afford the best

---

* It is but justice to confess that the writer of these lines having
become acquainted with the training-halter when he was an old
rider, was at first incredulous as to its value, but he soon became a
convert.

possible means of mouthing young animals. Training race-horses is so distinct and peculiar a branch of riding, that it seems almost presumptuous to offer even a suggestion on the subject; but we are quite certain that the halter here described would be of great value to trainers, saving them much trouble, and eventually diminishing the number of bolters and difficult starters very considerably, and thus giving many a horse a fairer chance than he would otherwise have. Of course it is not meant that the halter should be used otherwise than during the first period of handling; in actual running it would interfere too much with the animal's respiration.

The great value of being able to keep the horse's head in a proper position has been frequently dwelt upon in these pages. It is a matter with which almost every rider is acquainted, and the number of martingals, running-reins, and other contrivances invented especially to attain this object furnish an evidence of its great desirableness. Some of these are intended to act on the horse's nose, and are, therefore, nearly worthless; others again are fixed, and consequently more or less dangerous, besides requiring frequent alterations of buckles, &c., to make them suit; a third class act on the reins, and, interfering with the direction in which the pull on the latter is exercised, are wholly inadmissible; some few act directly on the bit or snaffle. To be really efficient, safe, and applicable under all circumstances, the running-rein or martingal should act directly on the snaffle or bridoon itself,* be wholly independent of the reins, and afford

* It is both useless and dangerous to interfere with the action of the bit by means of such contrivances.

a facility for adjusting its action, or altogether putting an end to it, without altering either buckle or strap, or even halting the horse if in motion.

As a general rule, when a horse has been once properly broken in and bitted, it should not require any contrivances of the sort : its use being continued after a certain period is an evidence of something being wrong.   Sometimes this is incapable of remedy, being a consequence of some peculiarity in the animal's build, and then there is no help for it ; but a good running-rein, possessing the qualities mentioned above, affords very frequently most valuable aid in the first handling, and will, if judiciously used, save the rider a great deal of trouble, the horse an equal quantity of ill usage, and, finally, simplify all questions of bits and bitting in a wonderful manner.

The best of all these contrivances hitherto invented is perhaps that known under the name of Seeger's running-reins (Schleif-Zügel), being perfectly simple, safe, and applicable to all styles of riding.   M. Seeger, the justly celebrated riding-master at Berlin, and undoubtedly at the head of his profession in Europe, first brought it forward.   It consists of three distinct pieces, the chin-strap, the running-rein, and the martingal.   The chin-strap consists of a leather curb furnished at each end with a small buckle and strap, by means of which it is attached to the cheek-rings of the snaffle or bridoon, the entire length, including the buckles, to be 6 inches ; these latter, when covered with leather, just wide enough to admit a strap $4\frac{1}{10}$ inches wide, and $2\frac{1}{2}$ long, projecting over the buckle, *behind which* it is sewed on to the body of the curb.   This curb carries a rounded strap in rear, supporting an ivory ring which may have an internal diameter of somewhat more than 1 inch (say $1\frac{1}{8}$), the external one being $1\frac{4}{8}$, leaving, therefore, the thickness of the ivory about $\frac{1}{2}$ an inch.

The running-rein is in one straight piece, $8\frac{1}{2}$ feet long from the buckle to the point, towards which latter it tapers off somewhat, its width being otherwise that of a common bit-rein, $\frac{6}{10}$ of an inch. An 18-inch strap of the same width is sewed on behind the buckle and pierced with five or six holes. The martingal has the same contrivance, as usual, of a buckle for forming a loop through which to draw the girths; but the other end of the strap (inch wide), instead of being split into two narrow ones, each carrying its own ring, is left of its full width, and carries one ivory ring of $1\frac{1}{2}$ inches internal diameter and $2\frac{1}{4}$ external, leaving, therefore, $\frac{3}{4}$ of an inch for the thickness of the ivory. The usual length of the martingal from the ring to the buckle is $3\frac{1}{2}$ to 4 feet, the latter affording scope for adjustment; and there is, of course, a neck-strap for carrying the martingal, which is too well known to need description.

Let us now suppose the horse to be saddled and bridled with a plain snaffle, the first step will be to buckle the chin-strap into the rings of the mouthpiece, the martingal having been previously put on in the usual manner, and its length so adjusted that the large ring it carries may just reach the level of the joints of the shoulders. The next step will be to buckle one end of the running-rein into a D ring attached for that purpose to the pommel of the saddle on the near side ; the other end of this rein is then carried forward through the ring of the martingal (from rear to front), from thence through the ring of the chin-strap from left to right, and back again through the martingal ring (from front to rear), from whence it goes to the rider's *right* hand. It is evident that a pull on this running-rein will act directly on the mouthpiece, drawing it back and somewhat downwards towards the horse's breast-bone; the great value of the whole arrangement being, that by taking the running-rein and right snaffle-rein into the right hand, and the other snaffle-rein into the left ditto, we can place the horse's head in any position we desire, and get a pull on the horse's mouth either horizontally upwards or downwards as may seem expedient.*

The training-halter offers no obstacle to the employment of this running-rein; indeed they may be very advantageously used in combination, and afford a most perfect command over the horse's head without the slightest approach to violence, and by slackening the end of the running-rein held in the right hand, its action may be at once put an end to, unlike all other contrivances of this nature, which are too apt to get hitched. †

The use of Seeger's running-rein for race-horses is perfectly unobjectionable. It gives the rider an immense power over his horse, which may be used momentarily, to check an attempt to bolt, for instance, and immediately relaxed, or it may be kept constantly in moderate action—for instance, with a horse inclined to throw up his head too high—and all this without in-

---

* The advantage as compared with other running-reins is, that the position of the horse's head depends on the length of rein grasped, and not on the force applied.

† Mr Childs, saddler, St Mary's, High Street, Bedford, has patterns of the training-halter and the running-reins.

terfering with his running; on the contrary, by using this rein one may dispense with sharp snaffles or curbed bits which so frequently have that effect. Seeger himself, however, thinks it unsuited to racing or hunting purposes.

But it is chiefly in the handling of young animals, whether for the saddle or draught, that these contrivances are valuable, because they enable us to attain our objects gradually and noiselessly, as it were, although with perfect certainty; above all, they afford us the means of avoiding all unnecessary violence, or any approach to ill treatment.

# CHAPTER IV.

WITH a plain smooth snaffle there is no question of lever action ; the amount of power applied to the reins is conveyed unaltered in quantity to the animal's mouth : to use a scientific expression, there is none of that mechanical advantage obtained which a mechanical power alone is capable of conferring. But if we combine Seeger's running-rein, which acts on the principle of a movable pulley, a certain amount of power applied to that rein will produce double the effect on the mouth that it would if applied to the snaffle-rein alone.

A still greater amount, however, of mechanical advantage may be obtained by means of a lever—and a bit furnished with a curb of a proper length acts as such. There are, however, several kinds of levers, and it will depend altogether on the manner in which the bit and curb are arranged, whether we obtain a lever action that is favourable to us or quite the contrary ; it is therefore necessary to say a word or two on the principles of lever action.

In the first order of levers the power is applied at one end, the weight being placed at the other, and the fulcrum or prop between the two, dividing thus the lever into two arms, a longer and a shorter one. The mechanical advantage obtained is proportionate to the relative length of these two arms. Thus, if $P\,F$, fig. 8 (*a*), be equal twice $W\,F$, a power equal 1 applied at $P$ will counterbalance a weight equal 2 applied at $W$; but, as regards our purpose, it is more especially necessary to observe that the power and the weight move in

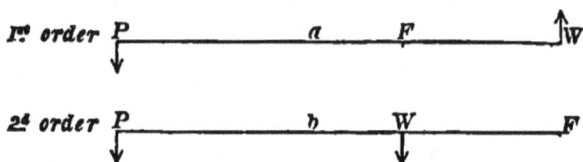

Fig. 8.

*opposite* directions, or rotate round the fulcrum or prop, as is shown by the direction of the arrows. Applying this to a bit, the bars of which represent the lever, there can be no question as to where the power is applied, being the lower ring to which the rein is attached, nor as to the direction in which it is intended to act, being towards the rider's hand; and if a bit act as a lever of the first order, the fulcrum or prop must be represented by the bars of the horse's mouth on which the mouthpiece acts, and the pressure of the curb on the chin would necessarily represent the weight to be raised. But it has been shown that, in levers of the first order, the power and weight move in *opposite* directions in their rotation about the prop; in this case, therefore, the horse's chin, in consequence of the pressure exercised by the curb, should move forward—that is to say, away from the rider's hand; and the greater the lever power of the bit, and the stronger the pull on the rein, so much the more would the horse be induced to stick out his nose,—an occurrence that is by no means infrequent, and at which some riders and drivers are very much astonished.

Now, in fact, there is no *weight to be raised* in the purely mechanical sense of the expression—it is a question of the infliction of a certain amount of pain from which the horse shrinks ; and if the curb act *more painfully* than the mouthpiece, in consequence of its construction or position, we obtain the action of a lever of the first order, which we should never desire. Some people are indeed regardless of the amount of pain they inflict on a horse, and go on increasing this painful action in both directions, without, of course, obtaining any real advantage, which is precisely what we would desire to see put a stop to ; and in order to this let us examine into the action of another kind of lever.

In a lever of the second order the power and prop act or are placed at the opposite extremities of the lever, the weight being between the two : the mechanical advantage is proportioned to the relative distances of the power and weight from the prop.  For instance, if $PF$, fig. 8 (*b*), be equal three, and $WF$ equal one, these numbers will express the relative amount of power gained; and it is to be observed that the power and the weight move in the same direction in rotating round the fulcrum.  This is what we want for bitting: the weight in this case is represented by the pressure on the bars of the mouth; the curb acting thus merely as a fulcrum, the horse's head follows immediately the pressure on the bar in the direction of the rider's hand.

It is very evident that the direction in which the bit acts depending altogether on the relative amount of painful pressure exercised by the bit and the curb, the horse's head will follow the rider's hand, even though the curb lacerate his chin, if only a greater amount of torture be applied to the bars of his mouth, the poor animal being left to deduce from the balance of pain what the rider's will may be. This is the system of bitting employed by the Arabs and other Orientals at the present day; our crusader forefathers borrowed it from theirs, and, strange to say, it is still more or less practised amongst us.

It is, however, quite possible to economise for ourselves all this surplus ingenuity in devising instruments of torture, and to spare our horses the infliction of it, merely by adjusting our bits altogether on the principle of a lever of the second order—that is to say, by converting the curb into a simple prop or fulcrum for the lever action on the bars of the mouth, which may be effected by rendering it perfectly painless, so that then the small amount of pressure exercised on the bars acting in the proper direction, and not being counteracted elsewhere, is the sum total of pain it becomes necessary to inflict, and even this may be reduced to a minimum.

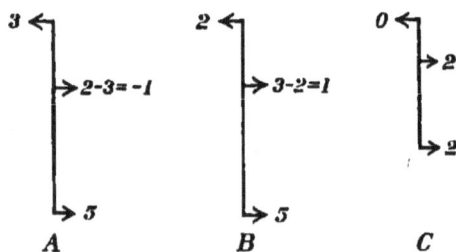

Fig. 9.

The adjoining fig. 9 shows that, supposing a power equal to 5 to be applied to the reins, it may, in consequence of various arrangements of the mouthpiece and curb, be made to exercise an amount of painful pressure as at *A*, where 3 parts act on the curb and only 2 on the mouth, which will make the horse bore into the hand; or as at *B*, where 3 parts act on the mouth and only 2 on the curb, so that 1 really remains available. Whereas, by reducing the painful action of the curb to 0, as at *C*, we find that the whole amount of action may be applied to the mouth, and therefore itself reduced to 2.

Here we have a key to the whole theory and practice of bitting, and there is no difficulty in understanding that its immediate consequence will be to render bits of small dimensions equally efficient and much more certain and reliable in their action than the monstrous pieces of ironmongery usually manufactured and sold ever can be : and we now proceed to enter into further details.

The first question that naturally presents itself is, the absolute length of the lever—that is to say, of the upper and lower bars of the bit taken together; the next, that of their relative proportions to each other. Before going into the consideration of these it will be well to clear up one or two preliminary matters, merely premising what is self-evident on inspection—namely, that a bit may be regarded as a pair of levers connected together by the mouthpiece. At first sight this might lead to the conclusion that the centre of the rivet on each side is always the point from which the length of the upper and lower bars is to be measured. This is however only true for those forms of mouthpiece which consist of a port and two lateral straight portions ; but if the whole mouthpiece form one curve, the line of

bearing—that is to say, the line connecting the two
points of the mouthpiece which rest on the bars of the
horse's mouth—does not coincide with the axis of the
bit passing through the centre of the two rivets, which
must be taken into account in estimating the relative
lengths of the upper and lower bars of the bit.—See
fig. 10.

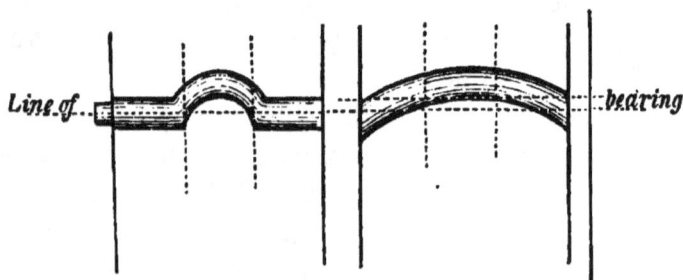

*Line of* .............................................. *bearing*

Fig. 10.

The measure for the length of the upper bar of the
bit, taken from the "line of bearing" to the point at
which the curb-hook acts, is the height of the bars of
the horse's mouth, which, as has been shown in a previous chapter, is pretty nearly a constant quantity—
namely, $1\frac{8}{10}$ English inches, decreasing with very small
horses and ponies to $1\frac{6}{10}$ ; therefore, rejecting *too* great
nicety, we may say *that* $1\frac{3}{4}$ *inches* is the proper length
for the upper bar—very seldom less, and hardly ever
more.

It would be very easy to demonstrate mathematically
why these two dimensions should always correspond,
but we prefer the simpler and more obvious way of
showing what the consequences of a departure from
the rule must necessarily be.

If one puts a bit into a horse's mouth *without attach-*

*ing a curb to it,* when the reins are drawn the bit turns right round, and its bars or branches come to lie in the same line as the reins.   There is no lever action whatever, because there is no prop, and a snaffle or bridoon would, on account of their centre joint, be much more efficient.   The same thing, too, will happen if the curb be *very* loose : the bit is then said to "fall through" —in fact, it is nearly useless.   The opposite fault to "falling through" is when the bit "stands stiff" without any play, the slightest pull on the reins causing the horse great pain, and, most probably, just in the wrong place—that is to say, externally ; for this stiffness or rigidity of the bit is very often produced by a *tight* curb, and therefore the horse, instead of following the rider's hand, pokes against it.   Good bitting will be equally removed from stiffness and falling through : it lies between these two extremes.

The length of the upper bar of the bit will, however, *of itself* cause this instrument either to stand stiff or to fall through, if it exceed or come short of the height of the bars of the mouth, as is shown in fig. 11, where *d e* represents this latter dimension, *d b* an upper bar precisely equal, *d c* one of only half the same length, and *d a* one double the same.   When a pull of the rein acts at *f* on the lower bar, the curb will be drawn closer to the chin, and the mouthpiece to the interior of that organ ; and supposing the amount of this "closing up" to be equal in all three instances, the bit with a long upper bar, *d a,* will assume the position *a' d f*[1].   It will be *stiff,* and the curb acting *upwards* in the direction *e a',* will press on the sensitive part of the jaw.   Moreover, there will be *no* lever action, the two arms of the lever being equal ; the

horse will therefore bore in the rider's hand.   On the
other hand, the bit with the short upper bar $d$ $c$,
equal half $d$ $e$, will assume the position $c'$, $d$, $f^3$—that
is, it will *fall through*.   The curb will no doubt
remain in the chin-groove, and act *forwards* in the
direction $e$ $c'$, but forming a very acute angle with the
branches of the bit itself, will have scarcely any value
as a *prop*.   The lever action, however, will be very

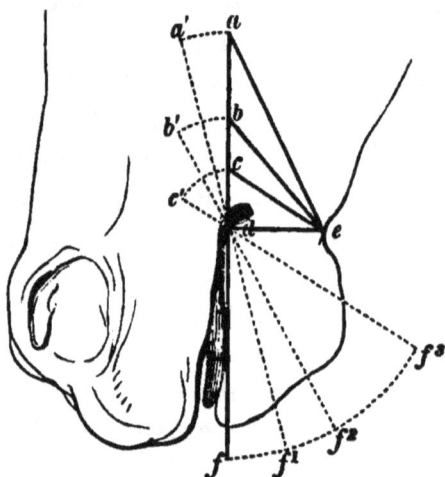

Fig. 11.

great, the lower branch, $f$ $d$, being to the upper one,
$d$ $c$, in the proportion of 4 to 1.   In fact, it will be
too great, and therefore reduces the prop to a nullity.

The intermediate upper bar $d$ $b$, equal $d$ $e$, will
assume the position $b'$ $d$ $f^2$; it will neither be stiff
nor fall through: the curb will remain in the chin-
groove, acting obliquely forwards in the line $e$ $b'$, and
will afford a sufficient prop or support ; and the lower
branch of the lever, $f$ $d$, being in the proportion of 2
to 1 to the upper one, $d$ $b$, there will be sufficient
lever action.

It will be now easy to understand how it comes that people, in order to prevent a bit with a very short upper bar falling through, are driven to using a very tight curb, the result of which is, that the whole action is transplanted from the interior of the mouth to the chin; as also that, in order to prevent one with a very long upper bar standing stiff, they use a very loose curb, which has the effect of making the bit fall through; and this—what is very common, nay, almost invariable in this country—an immensely long bit, is pulled up as high as it will go into the horse's mouth, and then a loose curb attached, and this great piece of ironmongery of course not only falls through, but acts nearly altogether on the exterior of the horse's jaw; whereas a much smaller and lighter bit, if adapted to the mouth, would be much more efficient.

Some portion of the objection to the long upper bar referred to above—namely, its affording no lever action —may be remedied by making the lower bar proportionably longer; and this is precisely what the ironmongers do, and, moreover, are encouraged to do by ignorant buyers. As has been already shown above, with reference to fig. 9, we are thereby driven to use much severer, that is, more painful, bits than are really necessary; besides which, there is another reason why we cannot go beyond a certain length with the lower bar. This is on account of the angle at which the rein acts on the latter.

We have already pointed out how much depends on the angle at which the power is applied to a lever, and that a right angle is the most favourable one for this purpose, which may be shown in a manner perfectly independent of theory. If the bit, fig. 12, were pulled in the direction *c*, it would evidently have no other effect than to pull it downwards, and out of the horse's mouth, if the headpiece of the bridle did not prevent

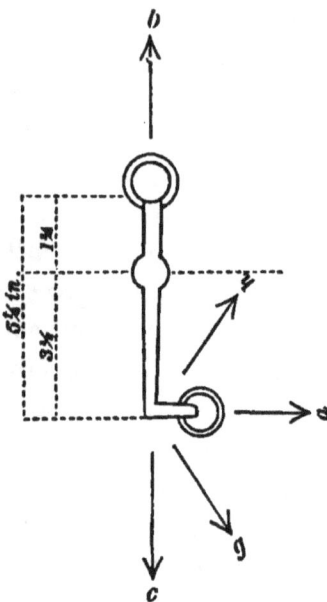

this taking place; and if the pull were made in the direction *b*, it would only lift the bit up till the angles of the mouth stopped it. In neither case would there be the slightest lever action; and the nearer any other direction, *g* or *h*, approached these perfectly inoperative ones, *b* or *c*, the less would be its value; and it is therefore evident that the direction *a*, which is equally remote from both, must be the most efficient —which is, however, precisely the right angle.

Fig. 12.—Angle formed by rein with bit.

Now a very long lower bar, or a very low carriage of the horse's head, à la Baucher, or a very high pack in the front of the saddle,* will always have the effect of bringing the rein to act on the bit at an unfavourable angle; and when we come to look at the bits that served as models for old equestrian statues, we find that the immense long lower bars of these were bent backwards so as to form an angle with the upper bars for the purpose of securing the action of the rein at a right angle, or nearly so—which, however, did not and

* See Plates VI. and VII., top figures.

could not answer the purpose intended.   If the invent-
ors of these frightful bits had had any real knowledge
of the laws of mechanics, and the application of lever
power, they would have found that the same amount
of useful action would have been much more certainly
obtained by a much shorter lower bar, without incur-
ring the very serious disadvantage of lifting the bit,
as it were, in the mouth, which always must have the
effect of causing the curb to mount up out of the chin-
groove, and therefore produce conflicting impressions,
tending to neutralise one another and puzzle the horse.
Moreover, the longer the lower bar the greater will be
the space through which the rider's hand has to move
in order to produce a given amount of action.   It will
be therefore slower, although more powerful, and consequently more unequal, rendering it very difficult for
the majority of riders to hit off exactly the precise
amount of pull required.

Having thus arrived at the conclusion that the absolute length of the lower bar should be diminished as
much as possible, and also laid it down as a rule that a
length of $1\frac{3}{4}$ inches is in all cases sufficient for that of the
upper one, it is not difficult to ascertain what the relative proportions of the two should be, which would, of
course, give us the absolute length of the former. And
here we encounter the only useful general rule that
bit-makers in general seem to be acquainted with;
namely, that *the lower bar should be twice as long as
the upper one*, which, increasing the lever action in the
proportion of three to one, should be under all circumstances ample.   But the bit-makers, although adher-
ing to this proportion, but too frequently make the
lower bar inordinately long, because they have no

standard of length for the upper one; whereas, if we adhere to the rule laid down above of $1\frac{3}{4}$ inches for the latter dimension, we have $3\frac{1}{2}$ inches for the former one, both measured from the line of bearing (see fig. 10), and $5\frac{1}{4}$ inches for the entire length of the bit measured from the point at which the curb-hook acts above to that where the lower ring acts below (see fig. 12). This will be the maximum required, and will be found to suffice in all cases; with very small horses or large ponies, the upper bar will have to be reduced to $1\frac{1}{2}$ inches, the lower one to 3 inches, leaving the total equal $4\frac{1}{2}$ inches, which will be about the minimum.

Some authorities, amongst these Von Weyrother, recommended the measured width of the mouth to be taken as a rule for the length of the lower bar: this varies, as we have already shown, from $3\frac{8}{10}$, $4\frac{3}{4}$ to $5\frac{1}{10}$ inches, and would be, therefore, somewhat more than the rule given above; but Von Oeynhausen adheres to this latter, and we are convinced that he is perfectly justified in so doing, because we have it in our power, by means of the mouthpiece, to effect the nicest adjustment that can be desired, and there is a much better chance of having the proper proportions adhered to by the bit-makers if we give them *one* or *two* fixed quantities, instead of a number of variable ones.

Next to the dimensions of the bars of the bit, the most important point to be considered is the curb; or rather, the position of the bit in the horse's mouth, taken in conjunction with the line of the curb, is what determines in the first instance the height of the upper bar, and consequently that of the lower one. *The curb must lie in the curb-groove, without any tendency to*

*mount up out of it on to the sharp* bones of the lower
jaw, otherwise, as we have seen, it ceases to be a
painless fulcrum, and renders the best constructed
bit uncertain, or even still worse, in its action.—See
fig. 11.

The only certain way of attaining this perfect pain-
lessness of the curb, on which so much depends, is—supposing, of course, this latter to be properly constructed
and of the requisite dimensions—by *placing the mouthpiece on that part of the bars exactly opposite to the
chin-groove;* it is only in this position that we have
the right-angled triangle, *e d b,* shown in fig. 11.    But
there is another reason for this : we find here the portion of the bar of the horse's mouth best suited for the
action of the mouthpiece—that space that intervenes
between the grinders and the tusks, where these exist.
With respect to the latter, it is necessary to mention
that there is great irregularity as to their position in
the mouth, some horses having them relatively higher,
others lower; nor do the tusks of the upper jaw always
correspond with those of the lower one, and mares
have very frequently no tusks whatever ; it is therefore
quite impossible to determine the proper place for the
mouthpiece with reference to these teeth, although even
the cavalry regulations continue to do so : the chin-
groove, in consequence of its relation to the action of
the curb, is the essential point to be considered.

Almost all the defects and absurdities of bits and
bitting may be traced to ignorance of, or inattention to,
this very simple rule.    A man puts a bit into his horse's
mouth—let us suppose that it is a well-proportioned one
in every respect; he fixes it at the prescribed "inch
above the lower tusk" if he be a soldier, or draws it

up into the angle of the lips if he be a civilian: he may just happen to hit off the right place, and if so, even an ill-shaped bit will work tolerably ; he is content with his work, and thinks he has mastered the difficulty.  But in ninety-nine cases out of a hundred the mouthpiece lies higher than it should; and if, in addition to this, the upper bar of the bit be, as it so frequently is, a quarter of an inch too long, then the curb mounts up out of the chin-groove and causes so much pain that the horse, to escape it, bores into the rider's hand.  He will then, perhaps, try a longer curb or a shorter one ; the bit will either fall through or be stiff, and he concludes that he must have a sharper one, and has recourse to some instrument of torture ; and so it goes on from bad to worse, till he gets rid of the poor ill-used animal.*

The best-fitting bit, even when placed in the proper place, will not work well unless the curb be properly constructed and exactly of the length required.  Taking all in all, a double chain worked quite flat, without prominent edges, and which, *when twisted up* to its full extent, *does not overtwist*, is the best kind of curb. Leather would be in some respects better than a chain ;

---

* This is no imaginary case : the author once saw a nice little thorough-bred horse at Ostend, and a few months later at Dublin, as second charger of a light cavalry officer of the garrison.  It was set down as an incurable bolter, and, passing through the hands of the riding-master, adjutant, and several officers, was finally sold as dangerous to ride, for £15 at a fifth-rate auction-mart.  The purchaser, a ladies' doctor, brought it to the author, who, after curing its dreadfully lacerated mouth and jaws, bitted it properly with a very light bit, which enabled the doctor to ride it within a week at a review of the regiment in question, and for several years afterwards, without ever bolting or being troublesome : never was there a better-tempered creature.

it is, however, not only perishable, but also subject to stretch or contract when exposed to moisture; and after having been once or twice thoroughly soaked, becoming hard and inflexible, it is more likely to injure the horse's chin than a well-made chain.

It is very clear that the narrower the chain is made the more likely is it to cause pain, which is just what we want to avoid, and we should therefore endeavour to make it as broad as possible. The vulgar notion of a sharp curb is, as the reader perceives, a monstrous absurdity. But there is a limit to this: if it be so broad as to fill up the chin-groove completely, there will be always a danger of its upper edge coming in contact with the sharp cheek-bones at every, even the slightest, pull on the reins, and getting up a sore which immediately interferes with the action of the bit; we must therefore select a curb that *does not altogether* fill up the groove. It is not easy to give any special dimension for the width of the curb-chain: eight-tenths of an inch will be found to answer the purpose very generally, but if we can use a broader curb without injuring the chin-groove, so much the better; it is more likely to be flat and painless. Curbs are frequently made to taper off a little towards the ends : there is no objection to this, except that, being more difficult to manufacture with precision, they are seldom so well made as the curb that is equally broad throughout. Single-chain curbs made of flat links may be good, if not too broad or sharp-edged; the plain double chain will be probably better made, and therefore preferable : the great thing is to avoid the infliction of pain; and if we are sometimes compelled to use a very narrow curb on account of the chin-groove being sharp and narrow, it will be well to have a cloth case to run over it, which may be taken off after use each time.

It is not possible to give an exact dimension in inches for the length of the curb ; a little reflection will show that it must always bear some special proportion to the width of the horse's mouth and the height of the bars, the latter of these quantities being nearly constant, whilst the former one is variable, as has been shown above. We must here anticipate, to a certain extent, the contents of the next paragraph. In order to render the action of the curb as painless as possible, it is absolutely necessary that it should press upon the greatest extent of surface that can be made available for the purpose, for which reason, of course, we require this instrument itself to be flat, and as broad as the chin-groove will allow. If the mouthpiece have exactly the same width as the mouth, the curb will wrap close round the chin, pressing equably over a large surface; but if, on the contrary, it be too wide, the curb will trend away right and left; and if the excess of width amount to half an inch or an inch, it will bear altogether on one spot and get up a sore,* although it is really longer than it should be.

It will be found that the proper length for the curb is about one-fourth more than the width of the mouth, the curb-hooks not being included in this; or, if we take these into account, the total of the curb and the two hooks will be once and a half the same dimension.

The curb-hooks form an important item in the ar-

* The author once found some thirty or forty horses in one squadron each with a little round ulcer on the chin in consequence of the bits being too wide.

rangement.  It was formerly the custom to have one
hook attached permanently at the near side of the bit,
and another of a somewhat different form to the off
side of the curb, but it has now become usual to attach
a pair of hooks of exactly the same shape and dimensions, which is a great improvement: the proper length
for these is three-fourths the height of the upper bar,
or about $1\frac{1}{4}$ inches.

The above length of curb applies to what is really
employed between the two hooks, but it is usual to
have one reserve link at the offside, and two of these
at the near one, which latter are convenient, or rather
indispensable, for catching a proper hold of the curb
when being hooked on.

We have now gone step by step through the several
details connected with the bit considered as a lever—
namely, its cheeks or upper and lower bars, and the
curb with its hooks, which represent the fulcrum or
prop.   There remains the mouthpiece, which is of
equal if not greater importance as the part of the instrument through which the immediate impression is
made on the mouth, and therefore generally placed
in the foreground by writers on this subject.   It appeared, however, to us to be a matter of great importance to make it perfectly clear, in the first place, that
the entire action of the bit should be concentrated on
the mouthpiece, that the operation of the curb should
be confined wholly to the function of a painless fulcrum, and that there are certain narrow limits to the
size of the upper and lower bars which form the cheeks
of the instrument.   The form and proportions of the
mouthpiece must be deduced wholly from the interior
conformation of that part of the mouth on which it

is intended to act, and these are, the tongue in the centre and the bars of the mouth on each side. It has been already pointed out that the relative hardness or softness of the mouth, so far as this depends on the conformation of this organ itself, is a consequence of the greater or less thickness of the tongue, and the greater or less sharpness and sensitiveness of the bars. The soft fleshy tongue is, of course, much less sensitive to pressure than the bony bars, covered only with a very thin membrane ; and consequently, if we used a perfectly straight unjointed mouthpiece of a moderate thickness, this resting wholly on the animal's tongue would, notwithstanding a certain amount of lever action, be the very lightest form of bit that could be well devised; in fact, a good snaffle would, on account of the joint, be more powerful. On the other hand, if by means of what is called a " port " we remove all pressure from the tongue and transfer it to the peculiarly sensitive bars, we obtain, with precisely the same amount of lever action as before, a much greater amount of power—in fact, the sharpest form of bit that it is generally advisable to use. Now between these two extremes there is a wide range, and the whole art of bitting consists, so far as the mouthpiece goes, in determining how much of the pressure shall fall on the tongue and how much on the bars, and we are thus enabled, by means of an almost infinite system of gradations, to obtain exactly the degree of action required in each particular instance by the nature of the service we demand, whatever the relative thickness of the tongue and sensitiveness of the bars may chance to be.

But there is one essential to be attended to—namely,

that the portion of the mouthpiece destined to rest on the tongue and the bars respectively should keep their proper places, and this can be secured only *by making the mouthpiece of precisely the same width as the horse's mouth.* For it is very evident that if a mouthpiece furnished with a port be *too wide,* a very slight pull on one rein will suffice to displace it, so that the bar at that side gets either altogether under the port, in which case the whole pressure is thrown on the tongue, or partially so, when the corner of the port will, by being pressed into it, cause great pain—in fact, the action of the mouthpiece, whether with or without a port, becomes altogether irregular and cannot be depended on. On the other hand, if the mouthpiece be too narrow, the lips are jammed in over the bars, the mouthpiece rests more or less on them, and the whole action is disturbed, besides which the horse is sure, sooner or later, to get ulcerated lips.

*The first grand rule must be, therefore, in all cases to make the mouthpiece precisely so wide that, when placed in the mouth, it fits close to the outer surface of the lips without either pressing on these or being subject to be displaced laterally.*

But it is also evident that the different parts of the mouthpiece must be exactly fitted to the interior of the mouth; that is to say, that those portions destined to act on the bars of the lower jaw should come into contact with them, and with them alone, and in the degree required; and that, on the other hand, that portion destined to act on the tongue should be of exactly the proper dimensions and form. Of course there is a great difference in this respect between smooth mouthpieces and such as have a port; in fact,

M

it is only as regards the latter that the dimensions are important. Where, then, a port exists, its *width* should be exactly that of the tongue-channel, as otherwise it would either intrench on the space allotted to that portion of the mouthpiece required for the bars, and produce the inconveniences alluded to above; or, if narrower, it would fail to answer the purpose for which it is intended, namely, to admit the tongue.* *The width of the port must be, therefore, exactly that of the tongue-channel*—and this is the second grand rule as regards the mouthpiece. Now it has been already shown that the width of the tongue-channel is very constantly three-fourths of the height of the bars, which, being equally constantly 1.8 inches, we have $1\frac{1}{3}$ inches for the maximum width of the port, even in cases where the total width of the mouth, and consequently of the mouthpiece, amounts to $4\frac{3}{4}$ and $5\frac{1}{10}$ English inches: for pony and hack bits, about 1 inch will suffice; whereas the common practice of the bit-makers seems to be to make it one-third of the total width in all cases.

For the height of the port, of course, no rule can be given, this being precisely the most variable dimension of all, and depending altogether, so far as the interior conformation of the mouth is concerned, on the relative thickness of the tongue and sensitiveness of the bars; and further, as we have already shown, on the temperament and general conformation of the animal; finally, too, on the description of service to which it is to be applied; to which must, in some cases, be added the

* The Germans call the port of a bit the "tongue-freedom"— *Zungenfreiheit*—which expresses exactly the purpose for which it is intended.

peculiar style of riding or driving of the individual that uses it ; for nothing can be more certain than that the best bitting in the world is wholly useless, nay, sometimes dangerous, in bad, that is to say, heavy or rude hands.

Fig. 13 shows a succession of mouthpieces of the forms now generally adopted, beginning with the lightest—that is to say, the one whose pressure is almost entirely exercised on the tongue,—and proceeding onwards with an increase of port or " tongue-freedom "

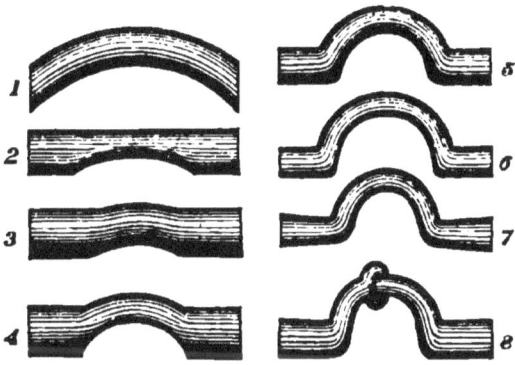

Fig. 13.—Various mouthpieces.

to the very sharpest it is advisable or can ever be necessary to use—namely, to one in which the height of the port is equal to its width, say $1\frac{1}{3}$ inches ; and beyond this it is impossible to go, because the slightest pull on the rein would, by altering the position of the lever, bring the top of the port to press against the palate, causing more or less pain, and therefore inducing the horse to bore with its head in the contrary direction to the pressure—that is, away from the rider's hand.

A mere inspection of these figures shows that the thickness of the iron or steel is an important item; the diameter of the straight portion of the mouthpiece may vary from a half to three-quarters of an inch; and it is scarcely necessary to point out that the greater the diameter the less painful will be its action on the bars of the mouth. When under half an inch it pinches to a certain extent, and should therefore be only employed when one is quite certain that this is desirable. In fig. 13 we have made the width of the port exactly $1\frac{1}{2}$ inches, that of the whole mouthpiece being only 4, which would be rather under the mark. The thickness of the mouthpieces Nos. 1, 2, 3, 4 is three-quarters of an inch, and these range from what is considered to be the very lightest form, No. 1, up to No. 4, which represents a medium bit. We, however, should always prefer No. 2 or No. 3 to No. 1, for the arched form of the latter throws nearly the whole pressure on the tongue, and the very small amount that falls on the bars of the mouth does so *laterally,* and not from front to rear. This form of mouthpiece, too, is always unsteady, and we have seen many horses whose tongues have been nearly cut through by its use with a tight curb. The mouthpieces Nos. 5, 6, 7 are only half an inch thick, which renders their action on the bars of the mouth more telling; they represent sharp bits. It will not escape observation that a greater thickness of the mouthpiece adds, in fact, to the height of the port; it is like placing an arch on higher buttresses, but it renders the action on the bars less painful, and enables us to meet the exigencies of special cases—as, for instance, where a horse has a thick fleshy tongue and very sensitive bars, and would not bear anything like sharp bitting.

There is another adjustment that may be occasionally employed with advantage, and which naturally finds its place here. The plane of the port is usually made to coincide with that of the whole bit; in other words, if we look at the instrument from either side, the port will be covered by the upper bars; but it is easy to perceive that, by inclining it a little forward, we may increase the tongue-freedom without making the port itself higher; this, however, can only be resorted to with a port of very moderate height, otherwise the roof of the palate would be endangered by every pull on the rein.

Again, we have the well-known contrivance of rings, which prevent horses from seizing the bit between their grinders, and thereby neutralising the lever action, as some will do occasionally; they are also very useful with what are called " dead mouths," and favour the very desirable process of " champing the bit." These rings may also be advantageously applied to the top of the arch of the port, where this, either on account of its absolute height, or its being inclined forwards, is likely to touch the palate. Where rings are employed they must be very movable, and, to insure this, few in number.

We have hitherto considered the mouthpiece as consisting of one piece, but fashion has introduced a great variety of jointed mouthpieces, and these are much used in England. We may classify these mouthpieces generally into such as, having a common snaffle-joint, are capable of being deflected in every direction; and, on the other hand, such as, having a hinge-joint, can only be deflected backwards and forwards relatively to the plane of the bit. In both cases the deflection

affords in its own way a certain amount of tongue-freedom, like the port of an unjointed bit; but here all
resemblance between the action of the two ceases; for
whilst the pressure, and consequently the action, of the
latter is exerted in a direction parallel to the horse's
backbone, that of the former, taking a diagonal direction towards the centre, degenerates into a pincer-like
gripe, which is wholly unreliable with the snaffle-joint,
and more or less so with the hinge one. From the
riding-school point of view, jointed bits are altogether
objectionable; from the military one, they are scarcely
admissible, although the Prussian light cavalry adheres
to their use. For road-riding and hunting purposes
the well-known Pelham is in great favour; and as
there must be some ground for this, it is worth while
inquiring into.

The great argument in favour of the Pelham is, that
the upper pair of reins give you the action of a snaffle—
which is, however, not quite correct, but let it pass—
whilst the lower pair afford that of a curb-bit, as the
expression is. To this latter we must oppose a decided
negative for two reasons: first, because the action that
results is that of a pincer, as shown above; and, secondly, because if the dimensions of the upper and lower
bars of our unjointed bits are very irregular and generally much exaggerated, they are, in the case of the
Pelham, simply monstrous, so that the curb is invariably dragged right up out of the chin-groove, and on to
the most sensitive part of the under jaw, the effects of
which we have so frequently pointed out. No doubt
the Pelham will produce "*painful* action" enough, and
so far those whose ideas go no further as regards the
unjointed bit are justified in making a comparison;

but a painful action exerted in a wrong or even uncertain direction is certainly a mistake.

If we had to address ourselves exclusively to really good and intelligent riders, we would say what they are themselves perfectly aware of, With your steady seat, and light hand resulting therefrom, you have more perfect command over your horses with a well-constructed snaffle than with any Pelham. Your very conviction of this sets you at ease, and that is a great point. If you want a little help with a young horse, here and there, or with one whose neck is turned upside down or the like, you have only to apply the running-rein or a martingal; or, if you prefer it, the same qualities of seat, hand, and *heart* will enable you to put a well-proportioned light unjointed bit into your horse's mouth. But the great majority of riders do not belong to the class we have described above, and having neither the steady seat nor the confidence that arises from it, therefore seek after something more powerful than the common snaffle. Indeed, as a general rule, one finds the bitting severe and the tackle complicated in the inverse proportion of the qualities of the rider; and as to a light hand it is altogether out of the question with people who "stick" on their horses after the fashion of a monkey mounted on a poodle, and derive their chief support from the reins. To such persons we would say, improve your seat in the first place : until you learn to keep it with ease, altogether independent of the reins, you will be always looking out for something Pelhamy that will afford you a gripe to hold on by ; just the very reason you can't master your horses with a snaffle, and, at a pinch, something with the action of a curb-bit, which you are

afraid of, because it affords little or nothing to hold on
by.  If your judgment were only equal to your pluck,
you would soon become independent of these hybrid
instruments that pretend to combine the action of
snaffle and bit, and, like most other makeshifts, answer
neither purpose perfectly and reliably.

We do not, however, mean to say that a Pelham
should never be used; as a matter of fancy, fashion,
or old habit, many a good rider will cling to it; but
then its dimensions should be as carefully adjusted
to those of the horse's mouth, and, moreover, to the
other peculiarities of the individual animal's build and
temper, as we have shown to be necessary with the
unjointed bit : and this brings us to another form of
jointed bit—that used, as already mentioned, in the
Prussian light cavalry (No. 8, fig. 13).

These are very similar to a straight-barred bit with
moderate tongue-freedom, but with a snaffle - joint at
the top of the port; and their dimensions being in
accordance with the size and character of the horses,
there is nothing irregular in their action, especially as
care is taken to put them into the proper part of the
horse's mouth.  We consider the unjointed bit to be a
better and more perfect instrument, especially in the
hands of a good rider; but we must not overlook the
fact, that the time of service in the Prussian cavalry
being restricted to three years, and, in consequence of
the system of recruiting, a considerable number of
men being brought into the ranks who have no previous habits of horsemanship, there may be reasons
for adopting this jointed bit quite independent of its
relative merit.

We would recommend those who, for hunting or

racing purposes, wish to have a sufficient command over
their horses, combined with a more decided leaning on
the bit than is necessary for road-riding or possible
for the cavalry soldier, to use what we should be inclined to call a dumpy bit, fig. 14—that is to say, one

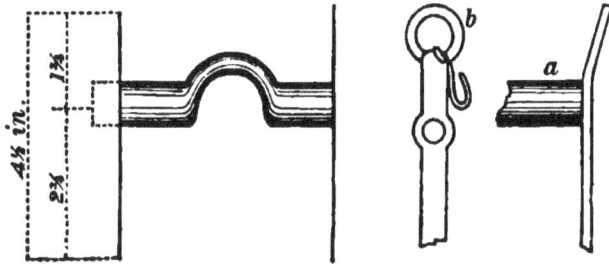

Fig. 14.

whose upper bar is exactly of the dimension prescribed
above, but whose lower bar, instead of being double
the same, is only about $2\frac{3}{4}$ to 3 instead of $3\frac{1}{2}$ inches
long, selecting some one of the mouthpieces, Nos. 2, 3,
4, or 5, fig. 13, that may otherwise suit, and placing it
accurately opposite to the chin-groove.*    Such a bit
would be found much more reliable than one of double
the dimensions that is badly placed; and although some
authorities recommend for such purposes an ordinary
bit placed a little higher in the mouth than its true
place, we have found it better to reduce the dimensions
of the lower bar, as you have *always* a difficulty with
the curb if you once depart from the rule.

We have hitherto treated the lower bar of the bit as
a straight line, and this is the form usually adopted
in common life; whilst for military purposes various
curves are adopted, the best and nicest-looking being

* A bridoon should be used with this as with every other regular
bit.

nearly in the shape of a capital S. This variety of form, it should be understood, has nothing to do with the action of the bit as a lever: the point of attachment of the lower ring, the centre of the rivet of the mouth-piece, and that of the upper ring or eye, should be in one straight line, and at the same proportional dis-tances from each other, in both cases alike. The real object of the double curve of the lower bar of the military bit is to prevent the horse from catching hold of it with his lips, and then getting it between his teeth, a trick many horses acquire. With the straight bar recourse is had to a curb-strap in such cases, as every one knows ; but it is much simpler and easier for military purposes to adopt the curved bar, and there is no other reason beyond whim and fashion why civil-ians should not do the same.

As to the upper ring or eye into which the headstall of the bridle is fastened, this is now pretty nearly al-ways really ring-shaped. In former times it was usually flattened down in various degrees from an oval to a mere horizontal slit ; but since the real principles of bitting have become better understood, the simple ring is preferred, and will be generally found to answer all purposes perfectly, although, no doubt, there are some cases where it might be convenient to use the oval-shaped eye ; these are, however, very few indeed. We have also hitherto considered the right and left side pieces (upper and lower bar taken together) of the bit as being in all cases parallel to each other, and conse-quently at right angles to the mouthpiece. There are, however, many horses, especially underbred ones, whose heads will be found to project laterally, immediately above the angles of the mouth, in a sudden instead of

the usual gradual manner; and the width of the mouthpiece is therefore insufficient to give the upper bars,
especially the rings, the requisite degree of play; or
rather, the latter will most probably gall the horse's
cheeks more or less.    There are two ways in which
this may be readily avoided; first, by inclining the
upper bars somewhat outwards (fig. 14, $a$), or by making
the upper ring movable (fig. 14, $b$), instead of its forming
a continuation of the upper bar.    Either of these methods will be found to answer the desired end, without
interfering with the proper action of the bit, and are
not only unobjectionable, but should be always resorted
to when necessary, because nothing is more common
than to see unthinking riders reject a bit whose mouthpiece has the proper dimensions, and adopt one that is
a quarter or half an inch too wide, simply because they
find that the upper bars do not fit *the outside* of the
horse's head; in fact, this is what frequently leads to a
wrong selection of bits.    People think of the outside
and visible part, and neglect altogether the much more
important interior of the mouth and the mouthpiece.

It may be useful to summarise here the whole of
what has been explained in detail in the preceding
pages.    We may say, then, that the average height of
the bar of the horse's mouth being $1\frac{3}{4}$ inches, the
upper bar of the bit need never be longer, except, perhaps, in very rare instances of horses 18 hands high
and upwards; and this gives us $3\frac{1}{2}$ inches for the
lower bar, and for both a total of $5\frac{1}{4}$ inches, measured
from where the curb-hook rests in the upper ring to
where the lower ring plays in its socket.    For ponies
or small hacks these dimensions must be reduced to $1\frac{1}{2}$
inches upper bar, 3 inches lower bar, and total length

of bit $4\frac{1}{2}$ inches.    These are the only fixed dimensions
that can be safely given; the remaining equally important ones are variable, and must be ascertained by
measurement in the way to be presently pointed out.

Let us now suppose that we have ascertained the
exact width of the horse's mouth, and also the proper
form of the mouthpiece; we then have the length of
the curb without hooks equal *once and a quarter* the
width of the horse's mouth, and the curb-hooks equal
in length three-fourths upper bar of bit, which will bring
the total length of curb *and* hooks up to *once and a
half* the same dimension; and it only remains to put
the bit and bridle in their proper places.

We have already shown how much depends on the
bit being placed accurately.    A quarter or even an
eighth of an inch higher or lower makes all the difference in the world.    The headstall or cheekpieces of
the bridle must therefore afford all the necessary facili-
ties in the way of buckles and straps for this purpose.
Military bridles and harness have nearly always two
pairs of these—that is, one pair by means of which the
bit is attached to the cheekpiece of the bridle by its
upper rings, and a second in the cheekpieces themselves, for the purpose of regulating their length; and
both pairs may be employed to determine the height
at which the bit is suspended in the horse's mouth.
There is a great inconvenience and disadvantage in
having a multiplicity of buckles, and many civilian
bridles—if we may use the word—omit altogether the
first-named pair, the cheekpieces being then sewed
directly into the upper rings of the bit.    This we hold
to be a great mistake, because, first of all, the bit,
supposing it to be of the proper size and shape, cannot

be so easily fixed in its proper place; and, secondly, it is impossible to change it for one that does fit accurately, in the contrary case.   In fact, this practice is evidently a consequence of want of clear views on the subject of bitting, and, on the other hand, a great obstacle to the attainment of the necessary accuracy. We hold the lower pair of buckles and straps to be indispensable.   The upper pair of buckles might be more easily dispensed with if one single buckle were placed on the top of the horse's head between its ears; for by means of this the total length of the cheekpieces may be regulated *generally*, and the *final* adjustment of the position of the bit accomplished by means of the buckles and straps, which latter should be pierced with holes at intervals of half an inch.*   Some people will, however, prefer the buckles in the cheekpieces; and if so, it will be necessary to see that they do not lie higher than the angle of the horse's eye, as they are otherwise likely to interfere with the position of the forehead-band, which should, like every other part of the bridle, including the throat-band, fit loosely, and cause the least possible amount of discomfort to the horse consistent with the object to be attained.

The noseband has pretty nearly altogether disappeared from our English bridles, which is also a mistake.   When horses have been once perfectly trained to the bit, and taken to it kindly, this strap may be dispensed with safely, if people do not like the

---

* It may sometimes be necessary to let the bit down or take it up by a smaller quantity than the half-inch affords: in such cases intermediate holes may be made; but the fewer of these the better, as they weaken the strap.

look of it; but, until this is the case, the noseband is
most valuable as a means of preventing the animal
from opening its mouth too wide and bolting the bit,
or catching hold of it between its teeth—in fact, evad-
ing its action in one way or the other. It is very
evident that we have by degrees got rid of the noseband because we did not understand its proper use;
and, when coupled with the monstrous bits we are in
the habit of using, it may have been found sometimes
a positive inconvenience; but any one that pays even
a slight attention to this matter will find the noseband
invaluable in the early stages of bitting. It must,
however, be put in the proper place—that is to say,
just across the nose at the point where the bone ceases
and the cartilage commences; and it should always be
buckled so lightly as to admit of a proper amount of
free motion.

We may now wind up this chapter with the rules
for placing the bit in the horse's mouth. When the
headstall has been adapted generally to the animal's
head by means of the upper buckle or buckles, the
next step will be to adjust the bit by means of the
lower ones, so that the mouthpiece shall come to rest
on the bars of the mouth *exactly* opposite the chin-
groove, unless, indeed, some irregular disposition of
the tusks should render this impossible, in which case
it must be moved *only just so much higher* as is absolutely necessary to clear the obstacle. The curb may
be then hooked in, first, of course, at the off side, leaving *one* reserve link, then at the near side, leaving *two*
such, and taking care that it lies quite flat in the chin-
groove, without any even the slightest tendency to
*mount* upwards when the reins are drawn. The curb

should never be quite tight; there should always be room for the first *and* second fingers of the right hand to pass flat between it and the chin ; and by gently pulling the reins with the left hand whilst the two fingers of the right are in this position, it will be easy to ascertain whether any pinching action occurs, in which case there is sure to be something wrong.

As to the measure of the proper length of the curb, we have already stated it *generally;* but each individual case will require a separate adjustment, and if the links be either very large or very small, it will sometimes occur that the difference of one of these will make the curb either too tight or too loose ; we must then, of course, try another curb.   If the bit is rigid or stands stiff on the reins being drawn gently, the curb will be too short; and on the pressure being increased, the horse will almost certainly either turn his mouth askew to avoid the griping action of the mouthpiece, or bear back suddenly to escape it altogether: we therefore give him another link, and drawing the reins gently as before, we observe whether, after the lower bar has moved through an angle of about eight degrees—bringing the mouthpiece just to meet, as it were, the interior of the mouth—the horse *gives* his head gently and gradually in the direction of your hand as it increases the pressure, without either poking his nose or shrinking back.   If this be the case you are all right ; but if the lower bar moves through a much greater angle than the above—say fifteen to twenty degrees—before the horse yields perceptibly, then your curb will be probably.too long.

We say probably, because you may, after shortening and lengthening the curb once or twice, find that the

horse will avoid the bit in the first case or remain in-
sensible to it in the second—in fact, you discover that
the mouthpiece is unsuited; therefore, in adjusting the
length of the curb, you must take care to avoid drawing your conclusions too hastily.  When you come to
a hitch of this kind, lift up the horse's upper lip gently
with your left thumb so as to get a view of the interior of his mouth, whilst you draw the reins with
the right hand so as to see how the mouthpiece lies,
whether too much or too little of its pressure falls on
the tongue—in fact, whether the mouthpiece is not in
in fault; but this requires some experience, and perhaps
the help of an instrument, of which we shall have to
speak in the next chapter.

   And now a word as to the bridoon.  This is, in the
first place, an aid in the early stages of training to
facilitate the transition from the snaffle to the curbed
bit; and in proportion as the young horse becomes
familiar with the latter it is gradually laid aside, and
then becomes a " second string to the bow " in case of
any accident happening to the bit or its reins.  Nothing
is, however, commoner than to see amongst ourselves
these its well-understood uses completely reversed, and
people riding about our streets and parks holding on
like grim death by the bridoon-reins, whilst those belonging to the bit dangle about the horse's neck, to be
caught up all of a sudden if the horse makes a bolt.
Now this simply proves that the bit is either so monstrous in itself, or so absurdly placed in the horse's
mouth, that the rider is afraid to use it; in many cases,
too, his own seat is so unsteady, and he depends so
much on the reins for support, that the best-fitting bit
in the world would be useless or dangerous in his

hands.   If those who really can ride would only bit their horses properly, they might take the bit-rein in their hands without any difficulty — nay, with great advantage to themselves, and we should see fewer broken knees than at present; for it is frequently owing to the slovenly way of shuffling along close to the ground, which horses ridden altogether on the bridoon acquire, that these are owing.   As to the other class of would-be riders, it will perhaps be better for them to take to the snaffle exclusively, if they do not prefer a Pelham, which we, however, do not recommend.

The bridoon being, as we have said, an aid, or " a second string to the bow," should never *interfere* with the bit; therefore it should be neither too thick nor so absurdly long as it sometimes is; and instead of hanging down in the horse's mouth so as to impede the action of the bit, it should be drawn up so as to fit *lightly* into the angles of the lips without disturbing the natural position of the latter: here it will be out of the way and still perfectly available when needed.

To conclude, *lightness, accuracy, easy motion, a total absence of stiffness, constraint, or painful action, are the characteristics of good bitting; and if these be attained, ready obedience to the rider's hand and heel will be the result.*

# CHAPTER V.

ALTHOUGH we have given above a certain number of permanent dimensions, or such as are nearly so, for the bit, there still remains a certain number of variable ones which must be. ascertained in each individual case—that is to say, the width of the mouth, on which so much depends ; that of the tongue-channel, nearly equally important ; and, finally, the relative thickness of the tongue, which latter, however, just because it is relative, is not susceptible of direct measurement.

For those who have had much experience in this detail, the width of the mouth, and consequently that of the mouthpiece, may be ascertained with sufficient accuracy by putting any bit that is not too small into the horse's mouth, and, whilst holding it gently *up* to one side of the mouth, measuring off with a small rule divided into inches and eighths or tenths how much of the mouthpiece, if any, protrudes beyond the side of the lips on the other side ; if we then deduct this amount from the actual dimensions of the mouthpiece we at once ascertain what those of the bit we seek should be : but it requires some practice to enable one to do this accurately.

Von Weyrother, formerly chief of the school of equitation at Vienna, invented a special instrument for ascertaining *all* the necessary dimensions, and this should be in the hands of all those who have any number of horses to deal with : we have named it, for want of some better word, the " mouth-gauge" (fig. 15, *A*).   This instrument is usually made of steel, and con-

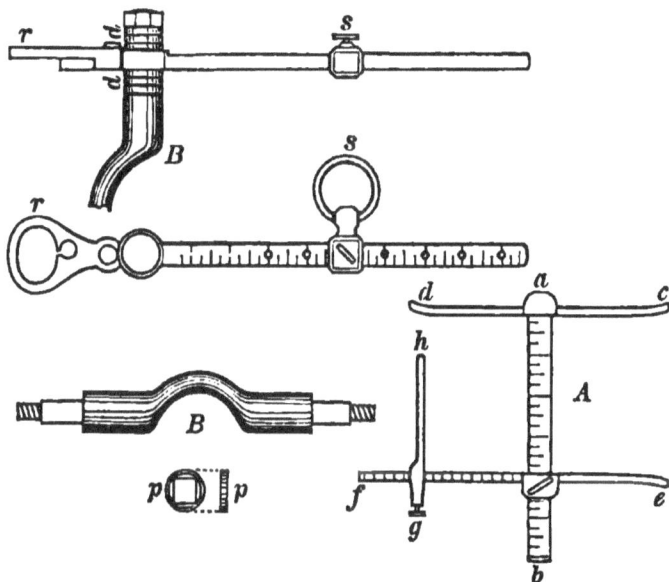

Fig. 15.

sists of a bar *a b*—about six inches long will suffice— fitted on one side at right angles with a fixed cheek- piece *c d*, of the form shown by the figure, and having on the other side a sliding cheekpiece *e f*, of the same shape and dimensions (six inches long), fitted with a screw for fixing it where required.   This bar *a b* is made oval in the transverse section, with the greater axis about one inch, in order to displace the lips nearly as the mouthpiece does, and is usually graduated throughout, but it will evidently suffice to do this with the fourth and fifth inches.

It is scarcely necessary to point out that if this gauge be placed in the horse's mouth like a bit, with the bar *a b* at exactly the proper point (opposite the chin-groove), the fixed cheekpiece *c d* being then held gently up to the off side of the mouth (the operator facing the horse's forehead), the sliding one *e f* may be shoved up just close enough to the cheek, at the near side, not to displace the lips; and then fixing it with the screw, and removing the gauge, we can read off the dimension of the width of our mouthpiece from the scale engraved on *a b*.

The figure shows further a rod *g h* fitted to slide up and down the movable cheekpiece *e f*, which is graduated into inches and eighths or tenths on its lower limb. This contrivance enables us to measure the height of the bar of the mouth, which is done in the following manner: The instrument, adjusted to the proper width of the horse's mouth, is placed as before, with the bar *a b* exactly opposite the chin-groove, but *underneath the tongue*, and is then wheeled round on its own axis till the upper limbs of the cheekpieces stand nearly perpendicular to the general line of the horse's nose. This, of course, brings its lower limbs in the opposite direction towards the neck, and the rod *g h* is then gently shoved up till it presses lightly into the chin-groove, taking care that the gauge stands square, and that the mouthpiece lies equably on both bars of the mouth. The rod *g h* is then screwed fast, whilst the screw of the cheekpiece *e f* is loosened altogether, so that the latter may be removed without

disturbing the rod $g\,h$; we then read off the height
of the bar on the lower limb of $e\,f$, and have all the
necessary dimensions.

It would be quite possible to take another measurement—namely, that of the thickness of the tongue, by
placing the bar $a\,b$ *over* that organ ; but it has been
already shown that it is its *relative* and not absolute
thickness we want to know; and that, moreover, we
must take into account the temperament and " build "
of the whole animal when we set about determining
what degree of relative pressure should be borne by the
bars of the mouth and the tongue respectively; so that
this proceeding would lead to no useful result.

Even those who have had most experience will
sometimes find themselves at fault if they rely merely
on measurement; and Lieutenant Klatte, a Prussian
instructor in equitation at Berlin, many years ago
invented for this very reason what is known as the
" trial-bit" (fig. 15, *B*).  This affords us at once the
means of ascertaining the proper bit for every horse
practically.  There are a certain number of spare mouthpieces which may be fixed in succession into the side-
pieces of the bit, their width being easily adjusted by
means of a number of small plates, $p\,p$, of one-tenth
of an inch thickness, removable at pleasure from the
inside to the outside of the side-piece ; and having
once ascertained the width of the mouth, we may
then, having also ascertained the height of the bars of
the mouth with the gauge described in a preceding
paragraph, proceed to shift the sliding ringpieces $r\,r$
till the upper bar has attained the prescribed length,
after which the curb with its hooks are fitted, and
then there only remains to slide the rein-rings $s\,s$ up or

down till the proper proportional length of the lower bar has been attained. Of course, as we go on from step to step with the adjustment, the straps of the headstall, and subsequently those of the reins, must be buckled into the respective rings ; and when, as a final step, the bridoon has been fitted and the curb hooked, the horse may be mounted and tried.*

In making this trial, those who have hitherto not paid much attention to the subject will do well to take account of the whole circumstances of the case—the temperament, build, &c. of the horse, the uses to which it is to be devoted, and whether it has ever been bitted before or not. If the trial-bit be really well adjusted, and the rider have a good hand, the horse will at once take to the bit, or at least give a promise of doing so, and nothing more will be required than to read off all the dimensions from the trial-bit, in order to have a proper one constructed; if, on the other hand, its action be found unsatisfactory, the lower rings, the mouthpiece, or the upper bar must be shifted till it does suit.

It should be borne in mind that the greatest defect a bit can have is to fall through or capsize—that is to say, describe a large circle before the horse shows itself sensible to the lever action. When this takes place to the extent of the lower bar forming nearly or altogether a straight line with the rein, there is no lever action whatever, and a good snaffle would be more powerful. This falling through may depend on the curb being too long, or on the upper bar being absolutely too short, or on the lower one being proportionately too long, especially in cases where the conformation and dimen-

* Mr Childs, saddler, St Mary's, High Street, Bedford, has patterns of the trial-bit and mouth-gauge.

sions of the mouth absolutely require a very short upper bar, when it may be necessary to make the lower one somewhat less than twice the length of the former, according to the rule we have given; but such cases are few in number, and must be regarded as exceptions —it seemed, however, advisable to mention them.

The next greatest fault is when the bit stands stiff in the horse's mouth; and this will be generally found to proceed from the curb being too tight, or the upper bar being too long, which latter always produces the third fault—the mounting up of the curb out of the chin-groove.

In conclusion, a word as to horses acquiring the trick of getting their tongues over the mouthpiece. This is a great inconvenience, as it renders the action of the whole machine uncertain. There is really no other method of cure except careful bitting and good riding, which may and often does by degrees lessen the evil, if not wholly remedy it; and these means will more frequently succeed with young than with old horses, *for it is almost always a consequence of bad bitting in the first instance.* Our advice would be to ride the horse for a certain time on a snaffle, and then a very carefully fitted bit may be put into its mouth with a fair chance of success; but there are some horses that never forget this trick when once acquired.

There is another trick which is not so inconvenient, although it is very unsightly—namely, when the horse lolls out its tongue either directly in front, or, as more usually happens, to one side. This, too, is usually a consequence of bad, that is, too severe bitting, and, with carriage-horses, of the bearing-rein being too short. In many cases a suitable bit will suffice, combined with a loose bearing-rein, where that has been the cause, and the horse will be immediately lighter in the hand. Sometimes, however, this fails, and the only remedy that remains is to attach a "fringe" to the mouthpiece, which, hanging down on the tongue, produces a tickling sensation that makes the animal draw back its tongue. However, we should be deceiving our readers in leading them to suppose that all cases are curable; for some horses will persist in this ugly trick despite of everything one can do. Any attempt to tie the tongue in this or the former cases will be found useless and probably dangerous.

Nothing is more certain than that every horse will go much better with a well-fitting bit properly placed than with the contrary; further, that many otherwise dangerous horses become perfectly tractable if properly bitted; and, finally, that inattention to this subject is one of the most frequent causes of restiveness. It, however, by no means follows that every rider should necessarily use a curb-bit. For hunting and racing purposes the snaffle will be generally preferable. Moreover, bad or indifferent riders had better not use the bit at all; but when, from whatever cause, it appears desirable to use one, let it be by all means a well-fitting bit, carefully adapted to the animal.

# PART III.

## RESTIVENESS: ITS PREVENTION AND CURE

# CHAPTER I.

THERE exist, no doubt, many horses that deserve the epithet vicious, in the proper signification of the term; they are, however, by no means so numerous in proportion as many people suppose, and it is of great practical importance that simple restiveness or disobedience should not be confounded with the peculiar temperament or disposition which constitutes a truly vicious horse. Such an animal's temper can scarcely be changed, although it may be dominated by force,—as, for instance, by Mr Rarey's method, which, by the way, was known to and practised by Major Balassa, of the Austrian cavalry, forty years ago; but the overawed and subdued brute is not thereby rendered a useful and docile servant, nor is any clue afforded us for overcoming special forms of restiveness or insubordination we may have to deal with: and so the horse-tamer, after attracting an undue share of public attention for a moment, finds himself in the end neglected and forgotten.

There is, too, a danger in all these methods—namely, the natural tendency they have to induce riders to rely on forcible measures in all cases, the result of which is but too frequently to convert a simply restive horse

into a decidedly vicious one, by awakening the devil
that slumbers within. *For it must never be forgotten
that in the end the horse is stronger than the man; that
there is very great danger of this becoming quite clear
to the former, when mere force comes to be opposed to
force; and that this very consciousness is what constitutes restiveness, and, if exasperated by cruel treatment,
vice, pure and simple.*

It is therefore necessary, in the first place, to know
clearly what one has to contend with—whether with
real vice, or merely with simple insubordination : the
former, if curable at all, can only be dealt with successfully by professional riders, who possess the proper
means and appliances; the latter ought to be within
the scope of a great number of horsemen, if they would
only abstain from violence and adopt rational methods.
The French say, when speaking of a horse that shows
restiveness, "il se defend"—he defends himself. There
is much truth in this expression, and it is one that
riders should constantly bear in mind, for insubordination is most commonly the result of something having
been demanded from the horse that it either did not
know how to do or was unable to perform; and the
very first step to be taken in all cases is, to endeavour
to ascertain exactly under what circumstances the disobedience was first manifested and is usually shown.

Before we affix the stigma of vice to a horse, let us
therefore consider for a moment what the poor thing
might with fairness retort, and the words ignorance,
timidity, or brutality will immediately suggest themselves; for, in truth, want of judgment as to what a
horse can fairly do, want of decision and promptitude
in demanding this, or unnecessary violence in enforc-

ing a demand, especially an unreasonable one, are almost always the first causes of restiveness. Mankind in its arrogance has thought fit to make the ass an emblem of stupidity, and why? Is it not because it seldom if ever opposes anything more than passive resistance to the tyranny of its oppressors? it wants the strength and the active courage that would enable it to act aggressively and deserve the title of vicious enjoyed by its near relative the zebra, whose indocility is not considered to be stupidity. We doubt much whether the horse is really more intelligent than the ass; it has greater strength and agility, and a more active courage, which, if it knew how to use, would enable it to set mankind at defiance equally as well as the zebra; and it argues a certain amount of stupidity when so powerful an animal suffers itself to be converted, as it often is, into the abject slave of a miserable taskmaster. The intelligence of the horse is, however, sufficient to enable it to find out very soon whether its rider be or be not deficient in that selfsame quality, or in courage; and, in the former case, the consciousness of superior strength encourages it to use this "il se defend"—that is to say, it sets the rider at defiance and turns restive.

There is another thing to be considered with regard to the horse's character—it loves to exercise its powers, and it possesses a great spirit of emulation; it likes variety of scene and amusement; and under a rider that understands how to indulge it in all this without overtaxing its powers, will work willingly to the last gasp, which is what entitles it to the name of a noble and generous animal. Now, whilst over-exertion, when unfit, will very frequently make horses refuse work, on the other hand, deficiency of exercise, and constantly riding the same dull round either alone or in company with other horses, will give rise to a whole string of evils ; as, for instance, refusing to go any but a certain way, or to leave their stable, or clinging to other horses they meet with, &c.; and this is just the reason why so many cases of restiveness may be traced to the stupidity or pig-headedness of a groom.   Horses don't like to be *ennuyé*, and will rather stick at home than go out to be bored ; they like amusement, variety, and society: give them their share of these, but never in a pedantic way, and avoid getting into a groove of any kind, either as to time or place, especially with young animals.   It is evident that all these things must be taken into account and receive due attention, whether it be our object to prevent or to get rid of some bad habit a horse may have acquired; and a little reflection will generally suffice to point out the means of remedying something that, if left to itself, would grow into a confirmed habit, or if attacked with the energy of folly and violence, would suddenly culminate in the grand catastrophe of restiveness.

The method according to which a restive horse has been originally handled must be also taken into consideration before one can form a sound judgment as to the best method of cure, as it makes an immense difference in this respect whether the animal has been treated on the English plan of merely gradually " habituating" it to go in the manner desired, and leaving it very much to its own will and pleasure to do so, or whether the Continental mode has been adopted of endeavouring to obtain, by more stringent and systematic means, a perfect mastery over its movements

in the first place.    Each of these methods has its own
peculiar advantages, and, as regards the prevention and
cure of restiveness, disadvantages also.    The English
plan is, no doubt, much less likely than the other to
lead directly to conflicts, simply because it avoids
them, but it does not afford that degree of control over
the horse's movements that is indispensable for combating insubordination successfully ; and if the horse
does slip into bad habits, the temptation to use violent
measures, which sometimes succeed, but as frequently
drive things to extremities, is very pressing.    In such
cases there is no other remedy than to commence the
handling *de novo,* which is a very troublesome and not
always successful operation, especially in the case of
aged horses, for such resist and very frequently resent
every attempt to gain that perfect command over their
movements without which a cure is hopeless, unless
the greatest judgment and patience be brought to bear
on them.    It was to English horses of this class, when
taken to the Continent, that reference was made in the
introduction to this little book.

On the other hand, the Continental or riding-school
system, aiming, as it does, at complete mastery over
the propelling power—that is, the horse's hind legs—
will, if hurried, or injudiciously employed, very possibly tend directly to call forth the spirit of resistance
and insubordination ; for it is precisely this control
over their hind legs that horses dislike and seek to
escape from with the greatest pertinacity and cunning,
and it is only by almost imperceptible degrees that it
can be attained, *when desirable.*    For the correction of
insubordination, it is, however, not only desirable, but
indispensable ; and it is therefore, generally speaking,

a comparatively much easier task to bring back truants originally handled in this manner to habits of obedience, than those that have been accustomed in their youth to the English *laissez faire* method.

It would be very easy, perhaps more to the taste of a certain class of readers, to lay down certain rules for this or that form of restiveness, and say, do this, if a horse rears, and that, if he rubs your knees against a wall, or insists on going home when you want to have a ride, but we have no faith in ready cut-and-dry receipts, and abhor all empiricism most thoroughly; moreover, there is plenty of it to be found, by those who prefer it, in most books on this subject. The real truth of the matter is this : whatever particular form of restiveness a horse may have recourse to " to defend itself," the one great patent fact in all cases is disobedience; and therefore the one great object to be attained is complete mastery over the animal's movements, and not merely over its body by means of straps and ropes.

We have stated that the English system of handling young horses is less likely of itself to produce insubordination directly, whilst the school system may, if abused, tend to this result. On the other hand, we must rely on the latter for the correction of restiveness; and the object of this chapter being to endeavour to show how vice may be *prevented and cured*, it seems advisable to lay before the reader a brief general sketch of both systems, pointing out, as we proceed, what is useful for our purpose in each, as also the means by which the one may be made to work into the other.

In the English method the first step is usually to put a very thick, and consequently very gently-acting, snaffle into the young horse's mouth, over which a

cavesson is placed ; a surcingle is then buckled round
the animal's body, to the rings of which, right and left,
the snaffle-reins are attached loosely, but still short
enough to keep the neck and head nearly straight, and
encourage the animal to *lean* on the mouthpiece.   A
judicious horse-breaker will then lead the young horse
about, at first in a quiet place, and gradually on to
roads, &c., where various objects present themselves,
as horses, vehicles, houses, &c., to which his pupil
becomes accustomed—a matter of great importance, as
many accidents occur where a young one that has
scarcely learned to tolerate a burden on its back is
brought, under a rider, all of a sudden in contact with
strange objects and unaccustomed noises.   Moreover,
the horse becomes habituated to follow the trainer, and
obey the lounge and reins in a gradual and gentle
manner, and a good understanding is soon established
between them.

And this, be it remarked, is a method seldom practised by school-riders, or in military establishments,
the consequence of which is, that the young horse,
when trained ever so completely in the riding-school,
has to undergo a new course of instruction when it
becomes necessary to take it out on the roads and
streets, and frequently gets into messes that undo
almost all that had been previously done.

Here, too, we find a practical hint for the treatment
of full-grown horses that shy at particular objects and
sounds, or object to passing certain spots.   Treat them
as the English trainer does his young ones, lead them
about as described above, and reward them for their
docility with a bit of bread, sugar, or something of the
sort ; you will thus avoid all conflicts, the danger and

o

evil consequences of which are enhanced a thousand-fold if you attempt to mount your horse under such circumstances.  Of course, when shyness arises from defective vision, which is often the case, this method will be of no avail.

But to continue : After a day or two the trainer puts a saddle on the horse, and the surcingle over it, and will then soon proceed to lounge it, which he generally does single-handed, a point to be borne in mind. For general purposes he will endeavour, by gentle means, to get the young horse to settle down into a trot as soon as possible,* and in proportion as the animal takes kindly to trotting, his trainer will shorten the snaffle - reins somewhat, so as to encourage the animal to lean more and more on the bit, taking care, however, not to make them so short as to prevent the horse stretching itself well out, and bringing the propelling action of the pasterns of its hind legs into play.†  This first lounging is always done on a large circle : first, because, if the horse does canter or gallop wildly, there is less danger; and, secondly, because the trot will be longer and more energetic, and the leaning on the mouthpiece more complete.   The object of this procedure is to encourage the horse to throw its weight well forward, go ahead resolutely, and use its hind legs altogether as propellers.   It may be well to give a caution here : grass land or clay, when trodden hard, if moist, is to be avoided—the danger of slipping is too great; sand or tanner's bark if available—if not, a piece of dry fresh-harrowed field—is preferable.

* The trainer of race-horses does not wish this, of course.
† We shall see further on that the school system demands this from the hocks.          •

There are certain forms of restiveness, or rather kinds of tricks, that insubordinate horses try on and succeed with, because they have never been brought to have a proper leaning on the mouthpiece, of whatever kind that may be.  For instance, they will get "inside" the action of the bridle altogether, so that the rider cannot keep them straight, and they will then turn sharp round and bolt off in another direction.  When, therefore, one finds a horse succeed in keeping permanently "behind the hand," as it is called, the safest and surest way of bringing it up well to the mouthpiece again is by a few lessons on the lounge after this fashion, aided by judicious demonstrations with the whip, and remembering to use large circles.

It will be unnecessary to go into the detail of the first backing of the young horse, and of the precautions that should be taken to avoid exciting its fear or anger ; and we therefore go on to the method of handling *under* the rider.  The great object all English horse-breakers have in view is, to bring their horses to go straight ahead and cover as much ground as possible ; they never think for a moment of making them handy, in the military sense of the term—that is to say, *capable* of circling to the right or left in all their paces, changing these and their feet without an apparent effort, &c.—for nothing of this is required of them. The methods they employ are, it must be said, perfectly suited to the object they propose to attain, the rider's weight being thrown either directly or indirectly on the horse's forehand, which, as has been shown in the first part of this work, favours progression on straight lines.  The saddle is generally for this reason put well forward, the girths coming round the anterior

part of the chest.   Now, although the saddle is placed
forwards, the stirrups being usually very short, the
body of the rider, from the hips upwards, is in most
cases farther back than the perpendicular line through
the fourteenth vertebra, fig. 4 ; but from the hips downwards the legs are brought forwards towards the horse's
shoulders, and the main reliance for the seat is with
that portion of the leg from the knee down to the
ankle, in the hollow close behind the horse's shoulders :
therefore, although the rider's body is actually farther
back than what we have described to be the normal
position, the direction in which his weight is thrown
by each impulse received from the horse's hind legs, is
diagonally forwards on to the fore legs, and not in the
vertical line shown by the arrows in fig. 4.   Moreover,
the rider's legs exercise in this their usual position all
the influence derivable from mere pressure, or from the
spur, wholly on the horse's fore legs, leaving the hind
legs free from all control, for they almost always come
too late when the rider endeavours to meet the horse's
croup or fix its hind quarters.

The system of bridling and bitting is also perfectly
suited to the object kept steadily in view, the horse's
head being kept low, if necessary, with the martingal,
which, of course, as has been shown, throws an additional portion of the weight on the fore legs.   When,
at a later period too, a curbed bit is used, this is put
so high up in the horse's mouth that the action of the
curb becomes more painful than that of the mouthpiece (see Part II. of this book), and consequently induces the horse rather to lean on the bit than yield
in the direction of the rider's hand.   Finally, this
latter is, both with the snaffle and the curb-bit, held

as low as the horse's withers will permit, and quite steady—that is to say, without much varying the pull on the reins. Of course a judicious breaker or trainer will endeavour to prevent his horse acquiring a dead hard leaning on the bit, and seek to restrain this within the bounds of a firm decided one. Under the circumstances, however, this is not an easy matter, and is precisely the rock on which so many riders split, who then have recourse to sawing, which frequently becomes the primary invitation to restiveness.

We may sum up the whole by saying that the English method of training young horses consists in doing the whole work on the forehand, leaving the backhand almost totally uncontrolled to perform the simple function of propulsion—for all the trotting and galloping work is done on straight lines; and there can be no doubt that, where merely go-ahead straightforward work is demanded, this system is perfectly judicious. It is, however, another question, and one already sufficiently entered into in previous chapters, whether its application be not too one-sided, for all saddle-horses are not required to do this sort of work; and it is positively objectionable in this respect, that it uses up the horse's fore legs with frightful rapidity, and to an extent that none but English purses can endure.

It is, however, with its bearings on the subject of the prevention and cure of vice that we have here to do. Now there are certain forms of insubordination, or restiveness, in which horses depend on their forehand—others again, and by far the greater number, in which they depend on their hind legs—for the purpose of defying the rider; amongst the latter we may

specify, for instance, rearing.  Considering the whole
rationale of the English system attentively, one is
therefore not surprised to find that the forms of restiveness in which horses use chiefly their hind legs
grow very naturally out of this system, which is unfit
for either their prevention or cure *without some further
aid*.   We would not be supposed to condemn this
system altogether, or unconditionally; on the contrary,
we have already pointed out some of its advantages,
and shall now proceed to show that it may be made
great use of, both as a preventive and remedy.  As
regards the former, for instance, it affords the only safe
means of utilising horses that have weak hind quarters,
or defects of the hind legs.  Many such animals would,
if treated according to the school system, be soon rendered either total cripples or incurably vicious; whereas, by a judicious application of the English method,
many a young horse gains time for the hind quarters
and legs to develop themselves, and becomes in the
end capable of doing even military work.

As to the cure of restiveness, the English method has
this value.  The first step to be taken with a restive
horse, before any attempt can be made at mastering its
hind legs, is to get it *to move somehow*, for it is only
when in motion that the rider can get at it.  Now,
although it would be worse than useless to attempt to
make a horse go under precisely the same circumstances
of time and place, &c., under which it has refused
obedience, still, by altering these circumstances, and
placing it under quite different ones, we can usually
succeed in this.  For instance, as has been already
mentioned, we can take a horse that proves restive on
the road into a ploughed field, and, lounging it on a

wide circle, compel it to go without risking a conflict of authority in which we might probably have the worst of it.   Or we may take the same animal into some enclosed space—a riding-school, for instance—where it sees that escape is impossible, and there, after having perhaps first lounged it, get on its back and ride it quietly.   Under such circumstances, to attempt to screw it into a particular form, or endeavour to apply school methods directly, would most probably end in a fresh display of insubordination, and we should find ourselves pretty nearly at the end of our tether, and without any further resource.   The great thing is to get the horse to *go somehow*—if only in a walk or a jog-trot, no matter: if we can only get thus far, half the battle is won, and by degrees we get into a good smart regular trot, if we take care to keep out of the corners, and avoid sharp turning.   Now the English method, as described above, is precisely that best adapted for getting a horse to cover ground, and therefore, for the purpose indicated here, it is like getting way on a vessel by means of the head-sail, without which the rudder is perfectly useless; after a while we can haul aft our sheets till we get a weather-helm and steer any course we please.   The English plan is therefore invaluable for getting way on, but to get a weather-helm we must have recourse to

*The Continental or School System.*—As the objects this proposes to attain are essentially different from what the majority of English riders aim at, so are also the means employed for the purpose.   Whilst the latter demand from each individual horse the greatest possible amount of speed on *straight lines* it is capable of affording—treating the question of wear and tear of the animal's fore legs as a matter of secondary importance—the proper objects of the school are : first, to fix on standards of speed and work attainable by the averages of various classes of horses ; secondly, to enable them to move with ease to themselves, and with the aid of the rider's one hand alone, on curved lines in various paces—that is to say, to make them handy; and, thirdly, to do all this in perfect obedience, and in such a manner that the inevitable wear and tear should be equally divided over all four legs, by which means the total period of service may be considerably prolonged.    In a word, the English system is based on the competition of individual horses on the race-course and in the hunting-field, and therefore employs the fore legs exclusively as bearers, and the hind ones equally so as propellers, speed alone being the object; whereas the school system, contemplating the simultaneous action of bodies of horses in varied forms, excluding altogether the idea of competition, and not aiming at the highest degree of speed, transfers a portion of the weight to be carried from the fore to the hind legs, establishing thereby a more equable balance of labour.    It is scarcely necessary to add, that the school is the nursery for military riding, which the hunting-field does not, and cannot profess to be.

The majority of English riders hold the school in the greatest contempt, simply because they are altogether preoccupied with their own ideas of the turf and the field, to which this is quite inapplicable ; and merely mechanical school-riders return the compliment with equal unfairness when they point to our broken knees, stiff fore legs, frequently exceptionally restive horses, &c.    It would be much more rational for both parties to endeavour to learn something useful from each other, for both systems contain much that is good and useful for all.

It is seldom possible for the school-rider to adopt the preliminary education of walking the young horse out on the roads, &c., as is the excellent practice of the English trainer, and therefore the remount is taken at once into the riding-school to be lounged.   The lounging itself, too, is carried out in a different manner, for it requires one or two assistants at first.   One of these carries the whip; the other, usually the groom, is necessary in the first stages for the purpose of leading the young horse round the circle until it knows what is required of it.   The assistant with the whip must understand his business perfectly—his services are most important and indispensable throughout.   As a matter of course, during the first lessons, a very wide circle is used, and the snaffle-reins are attached loosely to the rings of the surcingle, the *inner one* being slightly shorter than the other, as it would otherwise hang slack when the horse bends in the neck and body in circling.   The English trainer usually adopts the contrary practice of shortening the outer rein in order to prevent the horse running in towards the centre ; but this object is much better attained through the agency of the assistant with the whip, because the great object, especially in the subsequent lessons, is to meet and regulate the length of the stride of the inner hind leg by the inner rein, which, however, always must have a sufficient counter-pull in the outer rein—the isolated action of any one rein resulting merely in a change of position of the head, instead of acting on the whole side of the horse.

When the horse has become accustomed to circling

on the lounge in this manner with sufficient freedom, the trainer proceeds gradually towards his ulterior object of bringing out a perfectly clean, that is, equable and regularly-cadenced, trot, by accustoming the animal to transfer a portion of its own weight from its fore to its hind legs, without thereby checking its forward impulse more than is exactly necessary. This is easily done by gradually shortening the snaffle-reins ; and if the horse carries his head too low, by adding bearing-reins, for which purpose the dumb-jockey is useful. And now the assistant with the whip has the greater part of the work to do, it being his business, by demonstrations with that instrument towards the horse's *chest* underneath (not towards the hind legs), to keep the animal well up to its work, whilst the trainer himself moderates the pace by gently shaking the cord or line, never suffering the horse to lean heavily on his hand, and never himself taking a dead pull.

These two functionaries must act perfectly in unison, and both of them understand perfectly their work, which requires judgment, patience, and dexterity. Wonderful results may be obtained by a well-judged use of the lounge, but we are bound to say that, in unskilful hands, an enormous amount of mischief may be also perpetrated in the way of producing or confirming restiveness, or even with the more tangible evidences of curbs, spavins, and other lamenesses. It is impossible to give any precise rule as to the amount by which the reins may be shortened or the horse's head brought up. All that can be said is this,—if the horse hurries its trot, constantly increasing the pace, and finally breaking into a canter, you may be sure that the head is too low, and the weight still too much forwards, consequently you must bear it up gradually till this ceases.   On the other hand, if you find the horse trotting unequally and irregularly, in something like a mixture of trot and canter in an amble, or if it seems only capable of getting on in a short cramped canter, then you may be equally sure that your reins are too short, and you must immediately ease them all to the state in which they were at the very first lesson, and then try back till you bring out a perfectly clean rhythmic trot; whatever position the horse's head and neck may *then* have, is the true one, all the pedants in the world notwithstanding.   Indeed it is a good plan to finish each lesson and commence the next one with somewhat slack reins.   The being too lazy to take the trouble of altering the gear often causes double work, and a horse will bear more pressure, on the whole, with good temper, if you reward it by occasional spells of relaxation.

It will not be out of place here to remark, that if your horse be weak in the hind quarters or legs—that you cannot go so far with the bearing up, in fact—you must incline more to the English system; whereas if it has suffered only in its fore legs, you may carry the process to the utmost extent that is compatible with clean trotting; and this is precisely the reason why many an English horse, with ruined fore legs, may be rendered capable of doing good and safe service as an officer's charger for many a year, if handled judiciously after this fashion.

We now come to the period when the young horse has been saddled and backed.   The animal will, during the process of lounging, have become accustomed to the saddle being placed on the centre of its back and the girths round its proper waist, instead of round its chest. During the first lesson under the rider, the horse will continue on the lounge, the great object being to make the transition as gradual as possible, for which reason the assistant with the whip will continue his services, whilst the trainer also continues to direct the animal's movement with the line. The rider, therefore, will at first remain nearly passive, avoiding, on the one hand, interfering too much with the reins, and, on the other, pressing too closely his legs against the horse's body; in fact, his seat will be very much like that of the English trainer in the first instance, but by degrees he will take the direction of the horse's movements over from the trainer into his own *hands*, and with his *legs* do the duty hitherto performed by the assistant with the whip. For this reason he will then change his seat, bringing his legs well back so as to get a perpendicular tread on the stirrup, and holding them close to the horse's ribs without screwing. A slight increase of pressure of both legs *here in this position always* has the effect of making the horse bring its hind legs forward *under* its body, just as the whip does; and if, at the same time, the horse's head and neck are brought up and back, the relative proportions of weight to be carried by the hind and fore legs can be easily determined by the rider.

Let us now suppose the remount so far advanced as to enable us to dispense altogether with the lounge and the whip, and hand it over to the rider alone; in fact, to be in the stage of its education corresponding to that in which the English trainer takes it out for long rides on straight lines. The school rough-rider, on the contrary, does his work in an enclosed rectangular space,* which makes all the difference in the world, because during each circuit of the manege four corners have to be got through—that is to say, as many changes of direction made.   Let us take the rider, in the first instance, as being on one of the long sides of the rectangle, on which hand is immaterial : his English *confrère* holds his hands close together steadily down on the horse's withers, just *letting* the animal come up to meet the mouthpiece ; the school - rider, on the contrary, raises his hands more or less according to the natural position of the horse's head and neck, his object being, as we have seen, to bring their weight back towards the hind legs, which latter the pressure of his own legs tends to bring forward.   Moreover, instead of holding his hands merely passive, he takes a rein in each hand, and with a gradual but decisive turn of the wrist, *meets* each stride of the hind leg with a gentle pull on the rein at the corresponding side, working upwards and backwards.   Thus, whilst the pressure of the man's leg brings the hind leg of the remount forwards, the pressure of his wrist, exercised through the rein, determines exactly to what extent this shall take place, and, in fact, prescribes the point at which the foot shall be placed on the ground.   This is what is called floating or oscillating between the rider's hand and leg; it is what gives perfect control over the horse's movements, and explains why the terms " mere rein " or " mere stirrup " riding are used in a satirical sense.   A little attention will soon teach even a beginner which hind foot is being brought forward, and consequently with which rein he will have to regulate its action ; for it

* The circus, properly so called, is only used for purposes of exhibition.

will never answer the purpose to pull across, as that would only derange the position of the neck and head; and this "feeling in the seat," as it is called, is a sense that riders must cultivate, as it will enable them to find out *immediately* what their horse is about, and whether he be meditating mischief, which, if his leg be in the right place, he can nip in the bud; whereas, if it be somewhere away towards the horse's shoulder, he is sure to come too late.*

The corners and changes of direction must not be overlooked. At first these must be got through in a wide sweep, for which the lounging was sufficient preparation. By degrees, however, this sweep is narrowed, and the change of direction made more abrupt; we must therefore see how this is to be effected, and what results it produces.

When a horse moves on a segment of a circle, we must consider the two inner legs as moving on an interior somewhat narrower, and the two outer ones on an exterior somewhat wider curve. The difference between the two, although not very great, is nevertheless sufficiently so to compel the animal to shorten the strides of the inner legs perceptibly, and the shorter the radius of the circle, the more perceptible is this difference. When the rider is therefore about passing through a corner, he will come to the young horse's aid by urging forward the inner leg somewhat less than the outer one; at the same time he must bend the horse's neck and head in the proposed direction, and therefore he holds his inner hand somewhat lower than the outer one, makes his own leg at the same side more

* For the same reason it will not do to rise in the stirrups, English fashion, for we should miss each alternate tread.

perpendicular, the outer one being brought well back to sustain the action on that side. Now the result of all this is, that the inner hind leg is made to bear a somewhat increased proportion of the whole weight during the passage of the corners as compared with the straight line; and, thus by changing from one hand to the other, the young horse learns to bend his hocks in succession, and in an easy and gradual manner. After passing through the corner, and getting on again to a straight line, the action of the rider's legs is again equalised, but his hands always remain in the position described, as the horse's head must be kept slightly away from the wall or barrier.

This process is graduated thus: first, round off the angles in a wide sweep, then gradually narrower; secondly, halve and then quarter the manege, by which means the angles will come more frequently into play; finally, convert your smallest rectangle into a circle, and wind up by diminishing its diameter, changing, of course, from one hand to the other, in order to work both hind legs equally.

There are two distinct means employed here: first, the getting the horse's head and neck up and back—to use a nautical expression again, more inboard; secondly, to accustom the horse to bend its hocks and haunches so as to take over a portion of the weight. Unless greatly pressed for time, it is better not to commence both processes at once, and much preferable to devote attention, in the first instance, to the position of the horse's head and neck; and when some progress has been made with these, then go on to the hind legs. Therefore the seat and the position of the rider's legs will be at first more analogous to the English fashion, reverting, when the time comes, to the school position as a matter of necessity. A certain portion of the work of getting the horse's head and neck into position may be very advantageously done whilst the animal stands still, but no real progress can be made in getting it to carry its burden in the desired manner unless these bending lessons, as they are called, be immediately followed up by brisk trotting ones; and, for the same reason, it is of great importance, when practicable, to take the horse out of the school occasionally, and let it have a good straight-ahead go after the English fashion.

The dumb-jockey being much used in this country, it becomes necessary to say a word on the subject. This instrument represents a pair of hands without legs, and therefore can at best only perform just one-half of the work we have now under consideration, and even this imperfectly. We must therefore call the whip to our aid in order to supply the want of the legs, which the whip will do, but then we can never attain the alternately graduated pull on each rein successively, nor vary the pressure so readily. Moreover, the problem to be solved being the distribution of weight, with the dumb-jockey we can only adjust that of the animal itself, the whole of whose equilibrium being overthrown when the rider once gets on its back, we are then compelled to begin the entire process *de novo*. The judgment, tact, and power of appreciation of a really good rider will produce far better results, and, on the whole, in a shorter time than the dumb-jockey ever can do, except perhaps as a triumph of art in the circus, or for the purpose of combating some special form of vice; nevertheless it is evident, from what has been just said, that this instrument may be used with advantage by those who wish to train on the English system.  What we have here given is merely a sketch of so much of the school system as suffices to bring horses *into obedience*—in fact, the A B C of the method —as it would lead us altogether beyond the limits we have proposed to ourselves to go further than this into the detail of manege-riding, even if we felt ourselves competent to do so, which is far from being the case. Our object was to show by what means, within almost every rider's reach, perfect control may be obtained over the horse's head, neck, and hind legs, and this because it is by the aid of these members of its body, especially the last-named ones, that the vicious or insubordinate horse is enabled to defy its rider.

Up to the point at which we have now arrived it will have been most advisable to use a snaffle, either alone or in combination with Seeger's running-rein, which enables us, whilst we lift the horse's neck and head by the upward and backward pull on the snaffle-reins, to limit exactly the degree to which this elevation takes place.  When the neck, and with it the head, have been got into the desired position—which is, we repeat, always that in which the horse trots perfectly " clean" and in " obedience"—the next step is to get the head into its proper position with regard to the neck, and this is done by means of the curbed bit.

What sort of bit should be selected, and how it ought to be put into the horse's mouth, has been already fully explained, and all that will be further necessary is to accustom the horse *gradually* to this in precisely the way pointed out already for getting it to accept other limitations of its freedom.  If all this be

P

done carefully, skilfully, above all, patiently but resolutely, the result will be a horse moving in complete
obedience to the will of the rider, at all degrees of
speed, with perfect ease to itself, and without apparent
effort on the rider's part; for the animal will have learned
to modify the propelling and bearing action of its hind
legs in accordance with the pressure exercised by the
rider's legs, whilst the lever action of the head on the
neck produced by a properly-fitting and carefully-ad-
justed bit being transmitted directly to the anterior
extremity of the spinal column, and indirectly through
the medium of the reins towards the centre of *motion*,
will regulate the amount of action most effectually.
The two figures of Plate V. illustrate in different
senses what we have here endeavoured to convey by
words.   The upper one shows a horse whose hind legs
are subject to no efficient or direct control, the action
both of the bit and of the rider's legs being concentrated altogether on the forehand through the diagonal
tread on the stirrup and the pull on the reins directed
upwards towards the rider's neck.   The lower figure,
on the contrary, shows a horse whose body moves
under the perfect control of the rider: the tread on the
stirrup is vertical, the pull on the reins not far from
horizontal, and directed towards the rider's seat and
the common centres of gravity and motion.   Both figures sit nearly exactly on the same part of their respective horses.   The great difference between the seats
lies in the position of the leg from the hip, and especially from the knee, downwards; whilst the great difference in the carriage of the two horses lies in the respective positions of their necks.   Some of the other
plates illustrate the same thing in different ways.

# CHAPTER II.

THE first and most important rule to be observed is, *to ascertain the cause of the restiveness, and the circumstances under which it was first displayed and is usually repeated.* This alone will frequently suffice to suggest the proper remedy, as it will also show us how vicious habits may be best prevented, especially with young animals.

It is worse than useless to take your horse to the street-corner, the crossroads, the bridge, the railway crossing, or the house, &c., where it is in the habit of offering opposition to your will, as this only leads eventually to a trial of strength, in which the horse is always superior. You must choose a more favourable ground—namely, intelligence—in which man ought to be superior to the brute creation, which, however, by no means precludes the necessity of administering judicious punishment when necessary, and altogether excludes the idea of tamely truckling to the animal's insubordination.

The principal causes of restiveness are to be sought, either in some physical defect of conformation, in the condition of the animal, in its disposition, or in its temper, and sometimes in a combination of two or more of these.

With young animals especially, defects of conformation—as weak backs, hind quarters, or something abnormal about the head and neck—lead them into insubordination in self-defence. Want of ability to do the
work demanded of them, in consequence of defective
condition, will produce the same effect both in young
and old horses ; starvation is, therefore, in most instances, a positively injurious instead of a curative process. No doubt a horse's temper may be subdued to a
certain extent by this means, but then it becomes unfit
to do work, so that nothing is gained in the end. As
regards disposition, some horses refuse their work from
sheer sluggishness ; others, again, from timidity or irri-
tability. This latter is very frequently the case with
mares, especially at certain seasons of the year, and
may be very often remedied by putting them to stud
for one or two years. It is obvious that one method
of treatment is not applicable to these very different
cases. Finally, a merely passionate temper requires
different management from a dogged one; whilst sheer
vice is the most difficult of all to deal with, and usually
a consequence of injudicious treatment. When all this
has been well considered, and the cause or causes of
restiveness ascertained, one can begin to work with
some chance of success—otherwise not.

The second general rule is very easily deducible from
the first—it is this : avoid giving the horse an opportunity of resisting your will successfully, so long as it
possesses the means of doing so—that is to say, until
you have acquired, by the means already described, complete control over its movements. Therefore have your
horse led into a riding-school or some enclosed space
where it has never shown restiveness, and do your work

there, and after each lesson dismount again, loosening girths, &c., also caressing the animal, if obedient, and avoiding to push it prematurely to the verge of resistance, trusting rather to gradual progress than to violent measures. All horses are very susceptible to, and grateful for, kindness.

As an enclosed space is not always available, it will be well to point out what can be done without it, in case of necessity. Some horses refuse to leave their stable either from natural sluggishness or indisposition to leave their companions. A man on foot armed with a whip will often succeed in driving them away, but in this case it is his will and not yours that has prevailed, and therefore little real progress is made. It is much more advisable in such cases to lead the animal away to some distance, taking with you a nosebag with some oats, of which you give a handful now and then. You may after a time mount your horse, and when on its back give it a handful of oats from the saddle before attempting to go farther, getting its head, of course, in the proper direction. If you find this not to succeed at first, dismount again rather than risk a conflict, lead the animal out a couple of miles, and give it the whole contents of the nosebag at some convenient place, taking each day a different road, and never feeding twice in the same place. You may *always* ride home, and this will be your opportunity for acquiring control over its neck, head, and hind legs: the more it hurries back to its stable, the better will you be enabled to do this work.*

* It will be well to dismount at some little distance from the stable and lead the horse home, never repeating this operation in exactly the same place.

Or if it be a case of attachment to the stable companions, then put a rider on one of these, whose business it will be to keep sometimes alongside of your own horse, at others ahead, or again in the rear, making circuits, riding away and returning—the nosebag with oats may be superadded to this method of treatment; and thus the animal may be got and kept under way constantly, which gives the rider the desired opportunity of working it—for this is the main object to keep in view. Two or three servants riding together, and thinking only of their own amusement, will teach horses to cling to one another; or one riding the same dull constant round will stupefy a horse into restiveness, of which it may be cured by the above method.

But if you have an enclosed space of some kind to work in, 25 to 30 yards long, and 15 to 20 wide, it will be much better to use it in the first instance ; and then, when you feel it to be safe, ride out occasionally till the cure is complete. Of course your main object will be to get the horse to go *somehow* in the first instance, and then by degrees in obedience, the means of effecting which have been already pointed out.

Should the restiveness be traceable to physical defects—to weakness of the back, loins, hind legs, or to some peculiarity of conformation of the head and neck, as is especially the case with horses that seek to defend themselves by rearing or " bucking "—you must adjust your seat very carefully, and sometimes even change your saddle with that view. It is a great mistake in such cases, under the pretext of getting what is called a good firm seat, to rest your whole weight on the horse's loins, by placing yourself at one end of a long saddle, and tucking up your legs with short stirrups at the other end. On the contrary, one must get well down into the centre of the saddle, with somewhat of a fork seat; and the bringing your weight forward must be accomplished, not by bending in that direction from your hips, which will lose you all control over the horse's neck and head, but by bringing the seat itself into the proper place.

With irritable impatient tempers it is important to sit as steadily as possible—a close seat is what suits them best; they also require very careful and accurate bitting; anything painful exasperates such horses.

So, too, with horses that want to go; indulge them and moderate their fire gradually; whilst with sluggish ones encouragement will suit best; and as regards food, let it always be in proportion to the work, and this latter to the condition.

Of course it is impossible to lay down a ready cut-and-dry rule applicable to the treatment of each individual horse; but it will be almost always advisable to have recourse to the lounge in the first instance, if for no other reason, because it affords the best opportunity of seeing and studying the horse's action, and ascertaining exactly the means by which it resists; for instance, as is frequently the case, by slinking back from the bridle, and gathering up its legs under its body, and putting up its back at the same time. In such cases it will be best to continue the lounging at first on the English principle, and subsequently after the school method described above. If it seems advisable to get the horse's head and neck up, the dumb-jockey will be very useful; if, on the contrary, these require to be brought down, it will be useless; and with horses inclined to rearing it should never be used, on account of the danger of their throwing themselves down.

When one finds the horse inclined to trot out well and freely on the lounge, it will be time to get a rider on its back, and then to alternate the lounging and riding lessons as may seem advisable until the former become unnecessary. With *restive* horses it is, however, better not to attempt using the lounge after the rider is on the animal's back, but merely to detach the cord, leaving the cavesson on their heads, and giving the rider a pair of short reins, attached to this, into his hands, in addition to the snaffle-reins. Except in very skilful and practised hands, and when both trainer and rider are accustomed to act in unison, there is always great danger in using the lounge in this way.

The general plan is, therefore, simply this: first, lounging with loose reins; secondly, lounging with reins gradually shortened until the hind legs are brought under subjection, the horse still going free; thirdly, riding with loose reins; fourthly, riding with shortened ones, varied with bending lessons—at first whilst standing still, then in motion; finally, occasional rides out and giving up the school by degrees till it may be finally dispensed with altogether. Patience, determined cool courage, intelligence, kind treatment, and perseverance, are the main requisites; there is no royal road—the thing can only be done by fair work.

There are some horses that cannot be got to go *anyhow*, but will either take to backing, turning sharp round, generally on the near hind leg, rearing up, screwing themselves up against a wall, climbing up houses, or throwing themselves violently on the ground. Such animals have been usually brutally, or at least injudiciously, treated, and in most cases it will be advisable to hand them over to professionals, who should in common fairness be told the *whole* truth. A riding-school is, however, not always within reach, and we must therefore see what can be done with horses that have acquired vice to this extent.

The first step to be taken in such cases is *to restore confidence*, and make the horse feel that it will *now* be subjected to kind and judicious treatment. This must commence in the stable, and the foundation is best laid by the man who feeds and cleans the animal; and here let it be remarked, that an example of violence or severity given by the owner or trainer but too frequently induces the groom to follow it up, and should therefore be very carefully avoided. If, on the contrary, the groom succeeds in getting the horse to move about in his stall and turn round, a good foundation is thereby laid for the further treatment, and the trainer will do well to follow it up himself precisely in the same manner, giving the animal a handful of oats, a piece of bread, or a lump of sugar, which most horses are very fond of, whilst others prefer common salt. When you have got thus far, let the groom lead the horse out into a convenient enclosed space: at first it will be best to put nothing further on it than a snaffle, a surcingle, and a cavesson. When *on the ground*, the trainer may approach it quietly, and, giving it some tit-bit, make much of it, and then, with the assistance of the groom, fix the reins of the snaffle loosely to the rings of the surcingle, and firmly attach the line to the centre ring of the cavesson, carefully avoiding all compulsion. When this has been accomplished, gather up the lounge-line in a neat and regular coil in your left hand, so that if the horse makes a bolt it may run out without entanglement; and seizing the line about three or four feet from the cavesson-ring with your right hand, place yourself in front of the horse, the groom standing behind you.

Before proceeding further let us consider for a moment what position restive horses generally assume at the moment they defend themselves. In almost all cases it will be found that they gather. their legs under their body, sinking their croup, which may be seen from the position of the tail, getting their head and neck well down, and *putting* their back up like an angry cat. If the reader will now refer to Plate I., and compare this with fig. 4, he will at once see what the object of this position is. The horse's body is bent round the centre of motion (fourteenth vertebra) like a bow pulled to the archer's ear, ready to exert the whole of its elastic power. If the arrow be once discharged, your control over it is gone—so, too, if the horse makes the plunge it contemplates; therefore your first task will be to unstring the bow.

The first step to this is to get the horse to stretch itself. Try to get the head up a little; if you meet with opposition, give way, as if you did not perceive it, and try again. In proportion as you get the head and neck up gently the back will flatten down, and the horse will move one or both hind legs backwards, or one or both fore legs forwards. The horse does so merely to save itself from falling; you will do wisely by giving it credit for a first act of obedience, therefore pat its neck, rub its head, speak kindly, and give it something. If it has only moved one hind or one fore leg, by bending the head and neck gradually towards

the other one, this too may be got backwards or forwards: by degrees the horse will be got to stretch itself; the bow is unbent. It will altogether depend on
the time and trouble required to get thus far, whether
the first lesson should be further extended or not.
After a quarter of an hour or twenty minutes it will
be time to reward the horse by loosing all the straps,
leaving it to the groom to *lead* it about for exercise
and then home. Better take the trouble of giving two
short lessons each day, after which all parties remain
on more friendly terms, than one long one ending in a
fight.

Having explained at length the *method* of proceeding, it will now suffice to indicate briefly the successive
steps to be taken. When the horse has learned to
stretch itself willingly, the next object will be to get
it to move in obedience. If it refuses to go forwards,
by edging over its head and neck in the proper position, it will step sidewise to save itself from falling;
reward it again. In a day or two it will follow your
hand forwards for the sake of the oats you show it;
then by degrees it will learn to circle with the croup
round the forehand; you will "unfix" the feet and
flatten the back by degrees, taking care always to stop
each movement and limit its extent with the cavesson;
real obedience is thereby established, and the horse
will soon follow you in a wide circle, when, the assistant taking your place at its head, you at length arrive
at lounging, and proceed as already described.

A horse that backs — and some will actually trot
backwards—must be somewhat differently handled, but
still on the same principle : there is even less difficulty
than in the cases just now alluded to, because the

animal does move somehow. The position assumed by a backing horse is that described above ; the remedy is therefore to alter the carriage of the head and neck, getting these *up* as high as possible without violence, and the weight being more thrown inward, the back is flattened and the hocks bent instead of being stiffened as before. This soon brings the animal to stand still, which, however, should not be permitted ; on the contrary, it must be made to go backwards in obedience to the cavesson one or two steps, the head well up ; which done, reward it by suffering it to go ahead—and repeat this backing process until it goes willingly forward, when it may be handled as already directed.

In applying this method when on the horse's back, care must be taken to use each hand and heel (spur) in unison, "stopping" with the latter the backward tread of each hind leg alternately on the off and near sides, and not suffering the horse to put one hind foot to the ground too far away from the other, for one hock is then sure to be stiff. The pull on the rein must be, of course, upwards and backwards at the side corresponding to the hind leg you want to act on, and only upwards at the other side. If the rider hurries the horse back, fails to sit perfectly upright in the saddle, and makes a muddle of the action of his hands and heels, there will always be danger of the horse rearing up and falling back : in fact, this special form of restiveness is very often called forth by injudicious management of a backing horse ; whilst, on the other hand, making a rearer rein back *in obedience* is one of the best remedies we have for rearing.

To prevent misapprehension, it is necessary to explain how it is that the spur will stop the hind leg and limit its action, which is simply because the effect of the spur or heel being always to make the horse advance the hind leg at the same side when the animal is backing, this becomes, in fact, equivalent to stopping it; whereas, when it is going forward, the contrary effect is produced, and the stopping work done by the rein, as already explained in the preceding chapter.

It has been shown above that, with the cavesson, it is possible to lay the foundation for forward action by making the horse, in the first instance, circle with his hind quarters round the forehand. When mounted, precisely the same method may be employed with great success. The rider commences by lifting the horse's neck and head with *both* reins until the animal's mouth is somewhat higher than his own knee, keeping the calves of his own legs well closed on its ribs; then, by a gradual shortening of one rein, say the right one, he gets the head round till the forehead comes to be parallel to the horse's backbone, and places his right hand firmly on the saddle behind his own right knee, and so gets a *downward* pull on this rein, whilst with the left one he keeps the horse's head and neck in the proper position. Frequently a mere increase of pressure of the right calf will now suffice to unfix the horse's legs, and make it circle with the croup round the fore legs, which remain on the spot, and finally induce it to go ahead. Of course the outer, here the left, leg of the rider must be kept well closed up, so as to determine the velocity at which this circling is done, and the extent to which it should be carried, as also to be in perfect readiness to act in unison with the other leg, and with both reins, to determine the horse to move

straight ahead when it evinces the disposition to do so.
But still more frequently, perhaps, the pressure of the
calf will not suffice, and then one must use the spur
freely, and this will generally succeed.   Dead pulling
on the reins will not do ; the rider must increase and
diminish the pressure alternately, and always in unison
with the action of his own heels or spurs ; and this
latter should be screw-like—not stabbing or digging at
the horse's side, which involves a loosening of the hold,
and accustoms a horse to wince away or flee the spur,
instead of yielding obedience to the pressure of the
calf.   This is what the Germans call "wickeln"—that
is to say, winding or rolling up a horse—and, if properly done, is very efficacious for overcoming restiveness generally ; if employed in the nick of time, it will
even prevent rearing.

On the whole, it is evident that a key to the best
methods of mastering the horse's powers, and utilising
them fairly, whether merely for handling young ones,
or for the prevention and cure of restiveness, is to be
found only in a thorough knowledge of the mechanism of that animal's movements.   This we have endeavoured to explain in Chapter I., Part I., of this book ;
and those who will take the pains to compare what is
said there with what they see restive horses do, will
be thereby enabled to discover for themselves more
than we can pretend to teach them.

We would also venture to recommend the chapter
on " Seats" to the attention of rational riders and trainers, but especially of those who have to deal with restive horses.   In that chapter we could do little more
than hint at general principles so far as they are applicable to various kinds of riding ; here we can lay

down positive rules for the seat, and give reasons why it should be so and not otherwise.

We have seen how a horse that meditates resistance gets its legs under its body, coiling itself up, as it were, round one fixed point, the fourteenth vertebra. The nearer the rider's *seat* is to that point or centre of motion, the less will it be liable to disturbance from the violent efforts that ensue. If he sits further back towards the loins, his weight being there will interfere with his management of a rearer or a backer, and expose him directly to the action of a kicker; if, on the contrary, he sits close to the horse's withers, he unduly overweights the forehand, and loses most of his control over the hind legs. Let us compare together, for instance, the upper and lower figures of Plate V. on the supposition of the horses wheeling sharp round suddenly; those of Plate VI. on the supposition of their attempting to rear or kick; and those of Plate VII. on that of their attempting to back against the will of their respective riders. As to the hindermost figure of Plate III., selected purposely to illustrate an exaggeration, he can do nothing with his horse.

As regards the position of the rider's legs, the upper figure of Plate V. and the lower one of Plate VI. sprawl them out forwards, and the upper one of Plate VII. sidewise, with stiff knees away from the horse's ribs, so that they must *alter their whole seat* when they require to give the spur, which must be applied in this position with a stab, instead of growing, as it were, out of and being the climax of the pressure of the calf, the importance of which we have seen.

The position of the rider's body from the hips upwards is by no means indifferent. The getting up the horse's head and neck to the required position demands a certain amount of fixity of the spinal column, for the work to be done by the arms brings into play the muscles of the entire back.   The rider that comes into antagonism with his horse is only, then, safe in his seat when his own centres of gravity and motion fall in the same perpendicular line with the horse's centre of motion, otherwise he will have to contend with the centrifugal motion by dint of muscular exertion alone.

Now, for a man standing upright, the centre of gravity is in the perpendicular from the base of the skull, and the centre of motion is at the point where this line intersects a horizontal line drawn through both hip-joints.   If the rider sits upright, on his "triangle" (as explained above), and in the middle of his saddle, this being in the right place, his legs will, unless the stirrups obstruct, come of themselves into such a position that his own centres of gravity and motion will be directly over and very close to the centre of motion of the horse.   What Englishmen are pleased to call "a stuck-up seat" may be the result, perhaps, especially if the rider be awkward ; but it is not a question of taste or fashion, but of attaining certain definite objects which remain otherwise unattainable ; for no one will pretend that the position assumed by the hunting man for the purpose of making his horse throw its weight on the fore legs, with its head and neck well down *and extended,* can also serve the exactly opposite purpose we have in view in the correction of vicious animals.

A word with regard to the whip and its use will not be out of place.  The effect of this instrument depends altogether on the part of the horse's body to which it is applied, and the way in which it is used. One or two strokes given at the proper moment, and in the right place, will sometimes work wonders, whilst a severe flogging almost always does mischief. It has been pointed out that, in lounging, the whip may be made to do the work which the rider does with his legs and spurs, and that, for this purpose, it should always be applied under the horse's chest, about where the girth lies, and never to the buttocks or hind legs, as this usually ends in kicking. The same rule applies equally to the riding-whip ; but this may be also used to great advantage on the horse's shoulders—as, for instance, in cases where the horse is preparing to rear— the effect being to unfix its fore legs from the ground and make it put them forward, just as, when applied under the belly, it brings the hind legs in the same direction. Therefore it is absurd, when a horse defends itself by gathering its legs under it, to strike it under the belly, whereas one or two strokes smartly applied to the shoulders may probably have the effect of getting the fore legs stretched ahead. The promptness and rapidity with which the stroke is given, wherever applied, determines, to a great extent, its value ; for if the horse sees it coming, it will flinch away if possible, just as it does from a far-fetched stab with the spur ; and it can do this much more easily with the hind quarters than with its forehand, which is precisely the reason why a flogging—that is, repeated blows aimed at the same place—is generally useless, to say the least, whilst one or two on the shoulders tell at once. The manner of holding the whip or rod has much to do with this. We have often been amused at hearing would-be sportsmen turn Continental

Q

riders to ridicule for holding their whips or switches with the point upwards, as if they only wanted to imitate a sabre, whereas this is in reality the position from which a quick smart stroke on the shoulders can be most effectually applied; for if the point be held downwards, it must be first brought up, and then again down, so that it probably comes too late.

# CHAPTER III.

In the preceding chapter the general method of treating restiveness has been sketched in outline; what is there put forward will be found applicable to nearly all cases, and also suffice for the cure of most forms of disobedience. There are, however, some others which, in addition, require special methods of treatment, especially when they have become inveterate; and these are —bolting or running away, bucking or plunging, rearing, and kicking.

*Bolting.*—The first step to be taken is to ascertain *why* the horse bolts. A nervous and excitable temperament is sometimes the cause, and the only remedy will be quiet and judicious treatment. Much more frequently, however, bolting is resorted to by horses that have some physical defect or peculiarity of conformation, as a means of avoiding what gives them great pain; in fact, it is frequently rather an effort of despair than anything else, and an evidence that something has been demanded of the animal that was beyond its strength.

Fig. 7 shows the heads and necks of two runaway horses; in the one case the animal's nose is poked straight out—in the other, the chin comes back so as nearly to touch the breast; in both it escapes alto-

gether the action of the mouthpiece ; but the difference of position assumed points to a corresponding
difference of conformation.    The undermost figure
shows that the way in which the head is set on the
neck, and the build of both, offer no obstacle in themselves ; and the presumption is, therefore, that there is
something weak or defective in the loins, hind quarters,
or legs.    On the other hand, in the upper figure there
is evidence that such obstacles do exist in the head and
neck, the hind quarters being, perhaps, very powerful.
In a word, horses with short necks, narrow jaws, and
ill set-on heads, or, again, with long unstable necks, endeavour to escape the pain occasioned by injudicious
attempts to force these into a certain shape by running
away in the position of the upper figure; whilst those
with well-formed heads and necks will, if their hind
quarters be weak, usually adopt that of the lower one—
the getting down of the head alone bringing the weight
well on to the fore-legs, and consequently easing the
weak part.    It sometimes happens that there are defects at both ends, and want of judgment or temper in
the rider will easily drive such a poor weak creature to
despair ; for those who have had much experience with
young horses must have remarked that the powerful
and well-built ones seldom take to bolting unless there
is something wrong with their tempers.

The first impulse of the great majority of riders whose
horses bolt is, to put a sharper bit into their mouths,
or at least to shorten the curb, and perhaps rig the
horse out with some sort of martingal or running-reins
that gives them a good hold of the head, to secure
which more effectually they plant their feet firmly in
the stirrups, probably at the same time throwing their

own weight as far back as possible towards the horse's loins.   Energy is an admirable thing, but the energy of stupidity seldom avails much ; and the above plan of proceeding is nearly sure to make matters worse, and convert a terrified animal into a vicious one.   For whether the anguish the poor horse endeavours to escape from has its seat in the hind quarters or in the head and neck, severe bitting is sure to aggravate it, and a rude hard hand will do the same.   The best, in fact the only, remedy for a bolter is, a very carefully fitted and well adjusted bit, a perfectly painless curb, a light hand, and last, but not least, a very firm steady seat, somewhat forward with horses that have weak hind quarters.

It is always a good plan to put a bolter on the lounge, not, indeed, as is generally done, with the idea of letting it exhaust itself, for weakness is more frequently the exciting cause than strength, but for the purpose of studying carefully its action, and finding out by degrees in what position or trim it will go steadily and quietly in different paces.   The object will be, of course, with a horse that is weak behind, to train it on the forehand, getting its neck just sufficiently high up to prevent its being able, when the bit is applied, to bend its head round towards the hand, so as to escape altogether the lever action of that instrument; but, on the other hand, not so high or so far back as to throw the weight on the hind legs.   This will also afford a key as to the dimensions of the lower bar of the bit.

With a short-necked, narrow-throated, heavy-headed, perhaps straight-shouldered horse, possessing good serviceable hind quarters, the first object will be to get *these* to bear the weight gradually in the manner indi-

cated in a previous chapter.   This will, of course, require a higher and gradually ascending position of the
neck; but as the difficulty probably arises in the junction of the head with this part of the body, no attempt
should be made to bend the nose downwards, for that
is what annoys the horse.   The best gear will be a
bearing-rein like that used for carriage-horses, but with
the rings as close under the horse's ears as possible, so as
to lift the neck unbent at the part known as the poll.
In both cases the dumb-jockey is useful if judiciously
employed.

Subsequently, when the horse has learned to bend its
hocks, you may bit it with a light well-fitted bit, which
will bend the neck downwards without altering the
junction with the head ; in fact, what is technically
termed " a false bend " will be attained, which, however, suffices to render the animal controllable so long
as the rider preserves the mastery over its hind legs,
by keeping his own close to its body.   In riding such
horses, it is useful, when you find them beginning to
rush, to bring them *by gentle means* to stand still, throwing your own body, from the hips upwards, somewhat
forward, and easing the reins altogether for a moment ;
whereas the common practice of unskilful riders is to
throw themselves back and pull like grim death.

Reining back may also be employed, but not with
horses that are weak behind, nor otherwise than in a
proper position, so that the horse retires gently—the
contrary of backing, and never as a punishment.   Generally it will be preferable to stand still, and encourage
the horse, by feeling its mouth, to champ the mouthpiece, when the stiffness of the head and neck will
gradually relax, and it may be put in motion again.

Here it may be well to say what the rider should do if his horse runs away with him.   The general impression seems to be, that the safest thing is merely to endeavour to keep the animal straight till it gets tired of galloping, and keep one's own seat as long as possible; consequently the rider plants his feet as firmly as he can in the stirrups, and shoves these out towards the horse's shoulders in order to get fixed points from which he can have a *dead* pull on the reins, and of course his body, from the hips upwards, goes to the rear, right over the horse's loins.   Now, although this method of proceeding suggests itself very naturally, it is nevertheless all wrong, as, indeed, must be quite clear to those readers who have read the preceding pages with any degree of attention; for whether the difficulty has its seat in the horse's hind quarters, or in the throat and neck, it is sure to be aggravated in this way; besides that one can seldom reckon upon having room enough to try this experiment without encountering some obstacle, or a sharp corner, that brings horse and rider down with a smash.

Let us take the case of a horse running away in a field or open space, in the first instance, as being more easy to deal with.   Here the principal object must be to take your horse *off the straight line and on to a circle*—at first, of course, a wide one, but by degrees gradually narrowing.   On a circle one has room enough even for the tiring process, seeing that it never ends, but the thing is to know how to get and keep the horse on to it.   In the first place, then, it requires simply coolness and self-possession sufficient to enable the rider to sit well down in his saddle, bringing his legs *well back* and keeping his body *upright*—the legs being required *there* to regulate the action of the horse's hind legs in the manner already described, whilst the upright position of the body affords a basis from which the arms can work.   Next, instead of pulling a dead pull on both reins alike, the rider must take intermittent pulls on the one at the side he wishes to turn towards, gradually increasing the strength of the pull, and then as gradually relaxing to begin again; holding the other rein merely " counter," so that the pressure shall be exerted only through the mouthpiece, whatever the bit may be, and not through any other portion of it, which would be useless.   This intermittent pull on the rein must, however, be *always* accompanied by a similar pressure of the leg, or, if necessary, spur, *at the same side*, the rider's hand and leg acting in perfect unison; and this will never fail to turn the horse gradually, just as is required.   The circle affords, however, not merely an opportunity for avoiding dangerous obstacles; its great value is, that it also enables the rider, by gradually obtaining command over his horse, to demonstrate to the latter the utter futility of its attempt to get rid of him by running away, and that, too, without violence or severity.   One single attempt at bolting away, if taken advantage of in this manner by a judicious rider, may prove the means of effectually subduing a troublesome animal.   On the other hand, such a rider will abstain carefully from driving his horse to run away.

It is more difficult to manage a horse that runs away on the roads or in the streets of a town, because the rider is more or less compelled to follow straight lines. He can, however, unless the road be very narrow indeed, by using the rein and leg at each side *alternately*, compel the runaway to move on a serpentine, which is nothing more nor less than a series of curves alternating to the right and left, which will also enable him to clear dangerous corners ; one of these, indeed, if well taken, may possibly afford him an opportunity of gaining the mastery ; in fact, it will be found that most runaways are stopped after turning a corner.

The special management of the horse's head will, of course, in all cases, depend on whether it is carried too high or too low : if the former, the object will be to get it down ; if the latter, to get it up. The presumption being that the horse that runs away with its head up has no special defect in the hind quarters or legs, the rider may attack these more energetically, which requires his own leg to be in the right place, and the horse's head to be brought round somewhat to the same side. Now, although a dead pull downwards with both reins together will seldom bring the head down, an intermittent pull on one rein will bring it to one side, after which it will come down, the horse not being then able to stiffen its neck at both sides. With the horse that carries its head too low, the presumption being to the contrary of what is stated above, the rider must use his own legs more cautiously, and whilst he endeavours to bend the horse's head to one side with one rein, he will try to work it *upwards* with the other. This, of course, must be done with the bridoon if the horse be bitted, otherwise with the snaffle-rein ; indeed, it will be found that bringing the bit and bridoon alternately into action is preferable to using them simultaneously. It should be scarcely necessary to add, that the rider's weight must be always thrown somewhat into the stirrup at the side you wish to turn the horse towards, which is difficult when the stirrups are hung very far from the seat.

*Bucking or Plunging.* — In bucking, the horse gathers its legs under its body, puts its back up and its head down, and then commences a series of seesaw movements, throwing itself from the hind to the fore legs in rapid succession, either without moving forwards or in a succession of bounds, which latter, however, is more properly plunging. It occurs usually with young horses, and is much less common with English ones than with some foreign breeds, especially the Russian steppe horses. Sometimes very tight girthing, or too heavy a load on the horse's back, will cause it to buck; or the attempt to screw it up too suddenly into school form. The best method of handling young horses that have acquired this vice is on the lounge with the dumb-jockey, the great object being to get them to move forwards, and prevent the head coming down. As the bucking or plunging usually commences when the horse is put into a trot, it should be kept as long as possible at a walk on the circle, which is best effected by letting a man go alongside its head, holding the bridle, if necessary. The reins should not be buckled tight, as "forcing" a bucker will often make it throw itself down, or rear up and fall back. For the same reason, if it does begin to buck, just let it tire itself out, and when it is well wearied, one or two smart blows of the whip applied *under its chest* by the assistant will make it go ahead, and thus, by degrees, it will give up the habit.

If a horse takes to bucking or plunging under the rider, his object should be to make it go ahead by a few smart strokes of the whip on the shoulders, even at the risk of its running away, which he can meet in the manner described above; and this will even give him an opportunity of getting the head up, by first bending the neck to one side. It is, of course, absurd to sit far back on a bucker, sticking out the legs in front; a man that does so will be shot off over the horse's ears at the first or second plunge. The seat must be central, and the rider's back as straight as possible, although the natural tendency is to round it; the rider's weight, too, must be thrown "into his heels," right under his seat; this is the only chance of "sitting out a bucker."

*Rearing* is the most dreaded form of vice that occurs, and therefore the dodge that cunning horses resort to most frequently, as they at once perceive that the rider is afraid of it. Still it is by no means so difficult to conquer effectually as is generally supposed; no doubt a very courageous and cool-tempered rider alone can hope to succeed.

Rearing would occur much less frequently if it were well understood that it is almost always the last stage of disobedience, and very seldom if ever the first. In fact, its occurrence is evidence of injudicious management of some kind, either from untrained horses being brought into positions for which they are as yet unfitted, or from something being demanded of them that was beyond their power; or from the rider not knowing how to recognise and subdue the very first symptoms of disobedience; or, finally, from his using violent and intemperate methods of doing so.

We have already pointed out how bad management of a backing or bucking horse may end in rearing; but bringing a remount, or sometimes even an old horse,

into the company of other horses, and then trying to
get it away against its will, will often do the same; or
wanting to force a horse over a jump it does not like,
&c. &c.   Now, let us see what a horse does with itself
immediately before it actually does rear up.   The rider
is perhaps just congratulating himself how nicely he is
getting along, when all of a sudden he feels as if the
horse had collapsed under him; *his* seat is " nowhere;"
its head or mouth has shrunk away from the feeling on
the mouthpiece, and it has got its legs under its body,
and is come to a dead stand-still—the rider usually,
unless his seat be correct, falling forward with his
body, which of course makes matters worse.   Then
most riders will give a great dig with their heels or
spurs just anywhere they can get at the horse, or perhaps a blow with their whip, whereupon the animal
elevates itself on its hind legs, and becomes a rearer.
If the spurs, or even the whip, had been applied in
proper time—that is to say, before the horse came to a
stand-still—there would have been some use in them,
and it would probably never have come to rearing at all.
But if a man's legs are spread far away from the horse's
sides, and he thinks proper not only to dangle his reins,
but to sit with his back rounded in the so-called " knowing fashion," he will then have no " feeling in his seat,"
and is consequently quite ignorant of what his horse is
*going to do*, and of course must come too late with both
spurs and whip, if he happen to possess these imple-
ments.   An immense majority of rearers learn this vice
when being ridden about in a slovenly manner by
young riders or grooms; a man that keeps a lively feel
of his horse with both his hand and heels, and pays
attention to the play of its ears and to every variation

of its pace, will seldom if ever let it come to rearing, because the moment he detects the least slackness he will at once apply the proper remedy, which will be to make the horse come up to the mouthpiece at once ; but then his own legs must be well closed up to enable him to do so.

If you have ascertained that the trick of rearing was first practised somewhat after the manner described above, you may very reasonably hope to cure your horse without much difficulty.   The animal must be *led*, ready saddled and bridled, into a riding-school, or some enclosed space of convenient dimensions, in order to avoid giving it an opportunity for attempting dis-obedience on the way thither.   The rider will then mount, and begin by riding quietly round about at a walk, not as if he were merely wanting to see whether the horse would rear or not, but with the very distinct idea constantly before his eyes of getting it in the first instance well up to the mouthpiece, so as to have a firm leaning, recollecting always that this will depend quite as much on his own legs as on those of the horse ; after which he will proceed to correct the carriage or " form " of the animal in the way described in the introductory chapter to Part III., halting occasionally, bending the neck and head ; and, finally, when he finds that he *has* got a hold of his horse between his own legs and the reins—that is to say, feels that *he* is the regulator of the steed's movements at a walk—he may urge it gradually into whatever trot it pleases to go itself, and subsequently bring it into the form he him-self pleases ; in fact, he will re-train it till it is in per-fect obedience, when there will be no more danger of its rearing, under a *good* rider at least.

Should the horse, during this period of training, "try on" his old tricks, the rider must be prepared for it, watching its movements attentively, and especially all slackening or cringing in its paces, which should be promptly attacked, though not roughly. Acting merely on the defensive is quite out of place in handling vicious horses; one must meet them boldly. One or two promptly administered cuts of the whip over the shoulders will frequently nip any renewed attempt at rearing in the bud. With all restive horses, but more especially with rearers, it is essential that the regular seat should not be in the least disturbed by the necessity for using either whip or spur. A seat that may do admirably well for riding a willing horse over the stiffest country in England, may be perfectly useless for the sort of work described here.

Horses that have become confirmed rearers, and frequently thrown themselves back with the rider, will require great caution, and must be handled in a somewhat more methodical manner, though still on the same principle. We have shown what the horse does when it is preparing to rear; let us now for a moment look at it in the act of rearing. After slinking away from the rider's hand and seat, so that he loses all hold of it, the animal suddenly stiffens its hocks, throwing its whole weight on them, and at the same moment stiffens also its neck, and especially the throat, somewhat in the position shown by the upper horse in fig. 7, so that it becomes quite impossible to get a downward pull at it, and thus defies the rider most completely. It is always the same story—stiffened hocks and a stiff neck.* The safest way of managing confirmed rearers

* In the English method of handling horses little attention is paid

is on the lounge, *without* the dumb-jockey, which would be very likely to injure the horse severely in case of its throwing itself back.   Of course the reader will at once perceive that the general plan of treatment will consist in getting the animal to bend its hocks and neck in the manner already described above ; and we may, therefore, confine our observations here to what should be done when it actually does rear, which will be usually at the moment one attempts to put it into a trot on the circle ; for which reason bending lessons, when halted or at a walk, must be persevered in at first.   Supposing, now, the horse to be on the lounge, and suddenly to stop and rear up, the trainer, who must have an assistant that knows well how to use the whip, should shorten the line in coils in his left hand, holding it firmly in the right, just long enough to keep him clear of the horse's fore legs should it make a plunge forwards, and placing himself exactly opposite to the animal's head, so that, by stepping back a pace or two, he is sure to retain a good " feeling " on the line when its fore legs again touch the ground, the assistant with the whip stepping meanwhile smartly up behind the animal. The trainer should, in this position, merely keep a feeling on the line, as one would with a heavy salmon, never attempting to pull the horse's head forcibly downwards, or to jerk at the lounge, as the steady pull would only serve to make it lean on your hand and persist so much the longer in rearing, whilst a sudden drag is very likely to knock it over—a thing to be avoided if possible.   One must wait patiently, watch-

to the horse's hocks or neck ; whilst, on the contrary, the pasterns are severely worked, which is precisely the reason why school methods must be employed for rearers.

ing attentively the horse's movements, and taking care always to preserve his own position, so as to be ready when the moment for action arrives.  But the assistant with the whip should meanwhile deliver a few heavy deliberately - aimed blows on the animal's buttocks —not striking wildly, but taking care to hit one and the same spot repeatedly, and watching anxiously for the moment when the rearer shows signs of getting tired of standing on its hind legs, and is about to go down.   This is the moment at which the last and most effective cut of the whip should be inflicted; and this, too, is the moment for the trainer to give a short sharp drag on the lounge downwards ; and if the whip has been applied at the right moment, the horse will have been compelled to obey the lounge, the trainer's mastery will have been asserted, and if the horse ever again attempts to rear, during lounging, a very gentle pull of the cavesson on its nose reminds it of its previous defeat, and will probably insure obedience ; if not, the lesson must be repeated in the same manner.

Should one or the other hind leg appear to be giving way, as often happens, whilst the horse stands erect, the trainer should give a good smart pull on the lounge to the same side, which will throw the animal flat on its side, instead of allowing it to fall on its back, which is always attended with danger.  Sometimes, no doubt, a fall of the latter kind will cure the animal for ever ; but it is better, for many reasons, that the horse, having lost the power of maintaining itself and offering further opposition to the trainer's will, should be compelled to take the inevitable fall in the direction *he* prescribes.

Most horses, when they do at length consent to bring

their fore legs to the ground, especially if the whip has been vigorously applied at the proper moment, will make a sudden plunge forward, which is so much the better; the trainer must then step smartly to one side—the off one, if possible—and catch the horse cannily in mid-air with the lounge, handling it quickly and neatly, and taking especial care not to stumble into the slack coils in his left hand.   This manœuvre, if well carried out, will afford complete mastery, and render the animal perfectly obedient once for all.   All that remains to be done is to get the horse to stand still, the trainer shortening the lounge by degrees, and getting in front of the head, and the assistant placing himself behind the trainer's back, and putting his whip out of sight ; then "make much" of the animal, give it a handful of oats or a bit of something nice, loosen the reins and girths, and send it back to the stable.   Horses have excellent memories and sufficient intelligence to understand that they have been rewarded for obedience, and that their attempt at having their own way has failed.   This is a main point to keep steadfastly in view with all restive animals : avoid getting defeated yourself, and be kind and generous to the vanquished.   Of course this would only be a first step in the cure ; to make it perfect the horse must be re-trained or handled from beginning to end in the way already pointed out.

As it sometimes happens that a man is taken completely by surprise, a horse rearing that has never shown any previous symptoms of restiveness, it will be well to point out what should be done in such a case.   It requires presence of mind and great coolness, also a really firm seat, wholly independent of the stirrups on the one hand, and the reins on the other, to enable one

to deal with a rearer; but the thing can be done, and
without much danger, except on pavement or a slippery
surface, where it is better not to attempt a contest.
When the horse stops with the intention of rearing, it
first withdraws its mouth from the action of the reins
by getting its head more or less into the position shown
by the lower head, fig. 7; but when it begins to ele-
vate itself on its hind legs, it assumes the exactly opposite position, shown by the upper head of the same
figure, which, of course, equally enables it to defy the
action of the mouthpiece.   The advice usually given is
to slacken the reins altogether; but this is simply "playing into the horse's hand," because *its* object is precisely to defeat the rider's hand, first by slinking away
from it, and finally by resisting it openly.   Evidently
this advice is dictated by the apprehension that the
rearing up of the horse, depriving the rider of the usual
support of the *knees* and stirrups, will lead him to seek
this in the reins, and so pull the horse over backwards;
and no doubt this will prove correct for the great majority of riders.*   But if a man sits to his saddle by his
thighs, and has his own body in balance, there need be
no such apprehension; and if he then has only presence of mind sufficient to preserve a feeling with the
reins during the time the horse's head is passing from
the position shown by the lower to that shown by the
upper head, fig. 7, there will be a moment when it
will be in the intermediate position (see fig. 6, middle
head), and the animal's backbone will then also have
assumed an angle, not greater than 45 degrees, with

---

* The very fact of the horse ever getting the length of rearing is
presumptive evidence of the rider's legs being in the wrong place
at the time.

the horizon; the hocks, therefore, will be still bent somewhat (refer to Plate I. and fig. 4 to realise the mechanism of the hind leg).   This is the moment to screw both spurs as forcibly as possible into the horse's *sides*, the effect of which is, as we know, to bend the hocks, if the hand be held counter; therefore the animal will, in nine cases out of ten, make a plunge forward, and having preserved throughout a proper degree of feeling with the reins, the rider will be enabled to catch the horse in the air and bring it to the ground, so that the hind legs should touch this, if possible, a moment sooner than the fore ones, or at least so that they should get the greater part of the shock.   This is in itself a very severe correction, and one that *good* school-riders apply with great effect, with other forms of insubordination, not hesitating even to provoke an attempt at rearing in order to have the opportunity; if it be well done it may perhaps suffice once for all.

It may, however, happen that the horse has contrived to stick out its head (top one, fig. 7) and stiffen its hocks completely, so as to enable it to stand upright *before* the rider has made up his mind what to do.   Well, even then the game is not lost, if only the rider has a seat and patience to wait, just as in the lounging process, till he feels his steed coming down out of the clouds, which it is sure to do some time or another, when, if his hands and legs are right, he will be ready to act as described in the preceding paragraph on the horse getting down to 45 degrees.   In case the rider finds the horse actually falling, either directly backwards or to one side, let him throw himself off with a vigorous push of both hands so as to get clear. This we have done ourselves more than once; but the trainer misses an opportunity by being driven to this extremity.

*Kicking.*—There is a difference between kicking and kicking.  One horse will kick in harness, and not under a rider ; another will do just the reverse.  The former is probably extremely ticklish and sensitive to anything coming in contact with its hind quarters ; mares are frequently so, especially in spring.  The latter will probably have some weakness in the loins or hind quarters that is rendered painful when weight is put on its back.  When this vice proceeds from natural causes of this description, there is no help for it but to employ the horse in whichever way it is content to do its work quietly.  Again, one horse will kick at the spurs, another at the whip ; of course the exciting cause, whatever it be, must be avoided.

But something *can* be done with young horses that simply take to kicking during the handling ; very frequently the trainer has made some mistake, or been in too great a hurry, or put the saddle too far back, or girthed the animal too suddenly or too tightly.  All this should be, in the first place, well inquired into and ascertained, and the vice will disappear with its exciting cause.  There are, however, some young ones that take to kicking simply because they don't choose to go.  These should be put on the lounge *with* the dumb-jockey, which will prevent their getting their heads *down*, what a kicking horse always attempts to do.  If the horse stops on the circle and begins to kick, the trainer should proceed precisely in the same manner as with the rearer—that is, after shortening the lounge, and placing himself in front of the animal, simply wait patiently.  Meanwhile the assistant with the whip must place himself behind the kicker, and holding a sufficiently long whip in readiness, wait till the horse has extended its hind legs to their utmost stretch. *This is the moment* to apply a good stroke of the lash just under the animal's belly, taking care never to hit the hind legs, nor to strike at all except at the moment these are fully extended. The effect is perfectly astounding, and a few well-delivered strokes will generally make the kicker only too anxious to get away from the whip and go ahead quietly. Some horses will, however, when baffled in this way, cease kicking, but still refuse to move forward. The trainer must then proceed to "unfix their feet" in the manner described in Chapter II. Part III., or make them rein back gradually. Other horses will perhaps take to "running" backwards. All one can then do is to follow them quietly, merely keeping their heads straight, so that they should not run up against a wall or the like, but always taking care not to press so heavily on the lounge as to throw the animal's weight *on* the fore legs, as this, of course, will be a good opportunity to renew the kicking. When the horse gets tired of backing it will stop of its own accord. This moment must be attentively watched for by the assistant with the whip, who should then "pitch in" a dexterous stroke under the belly, and this will generally suffice to get the animal to go forwards.

In conclusion, it cannot be too strongly impressed on the minds of those who undertake to handle restive horses, that very little can be done by main force, nothing at all by cruel or even severe treatment, whereas everything may be fairly hoped from patience, judg-

ment, and kindness. It is especially in this department of riding that the truth of our Horatian motto,
"Vis consili expers mole ruit suâ," verifies itself.
One can almost fancy that the passage was suggested
to the Latin poet by having seen some Roman rough-
rider dragging a rearing horse over on himself.

# INDEX.

# INDEX.

THE END.

PRINTED BY WILLIAM BLACKWOOD AND SONS, EDINBURGH.